YEVTUSHENKO'S READER

Also by Yevgeny Yevtushenko
(in English)

YEVTUSHENKO'S READER

The Spirit of Elbe
A Precocious Autobiography
Poems

BY YEVGENY YEVTUSHENKO

English Translations:

ROBIN MILNER-GULLAND AND PETER LEVI, S. J.
ANDREW R. MacANDREW
GEORGE REAVEY
ALBERT C. TODD
JOHN UPDIKE
STANLEY KUNITZ
VERA DUNHAM
HERBERT MARSHALL

E. P. DUTTON & CO., INC.   NEW YORK   1972

CONTENTS

THE SPIRIT OF ELBE

(To My American Readers)

Sometime in 1945, Russian and American soldiers met on the River Elbe. As they sailed to meet each other over its spring waters, they waved weapons and flasks of whisky and vodka.

They embraced, drank, sang, fired into the air, and showed each other tattered photographs of their sweethearts, wives, and children.

The future of those children, smiling from the photographs, seemed to these soldiers to be one of untroubled peace, now and forever.

Our feelings toward a common enemy gave birth in us to feelings of a common goal.

But there came people who transformed victory over a common enemy into a means of disuniting, instead of uniting us even more closely. Cursed be those cynics who for so many years strove to kill in our hearts the sacred spirit of Elbe.

Yet, despite them, the spirit of Elbe lives on in the hearts of our peoples, for all people have the same enemies—in peace and in war: militarists, spies, exploiters, nationalists, stiflers of honor, goodness, and justice. Let these feelings toward our common enemies create for us a common goal, as once it did on the River Elbe. . .

For the aim of all working people the world over is one, no matter how they may differ as to the means of achieving it: freedom, equality, and universal brotherhood.

The achievement of this aim depends, of course, on the interrelationships of all peoples—big and small—but tremendously important is the kind of relationship that exists between us—Russians and Americans.

Differences in political systems should not prevent our peoples living in peace and friendship, for in our friendship lies the only possibility of achieving a peaceful future for our children. Any militant opponent of friendship with the Russians—no matter with what pro-American phrases he may mask himself—is objectively an anti-American, for he menaces the whole future of his people.

In the final analysis, humanity has only two ways out—either universal destruction or universal brotherhood. Both right-wing and left-wing phrases about the impossibility of peaceful co-existence of countries with different systems are criminal, even if they arise simply out of thoughtlessness.

"A friend in need is a friend indeed." So in the relationships between peoples.

When America was struck with a national misfortune—the villainous murder of Kennedy—we were all profoundly shocked and shared America's own unhappiness.

This is convincing enough proof that our peoples are not only obliged to, but *can* understand and feel for each other.

Of course it is a good thing that there is direct communication between the Kremlin and the White House via the "Hot Line" and that diplomatic, commercial, and tourist contacts increase still more. But a tremendous part in strengthening friendship between our peoples must be played by art, whose eternal role is the uniting of human hearts in the name of goodness and justice.

Pushkin, Tolstoy, Chekhov, Dostoyevsky, Gogol, Gorki,

Mayakovsky, Pasternak, and the books of many others of our writers standing on the bookshelves of American homes, carried on this good work. The publication in the United States of the books of Solzhenitsyn, Kazakov, Voznesensky, and other contemporary Soviet writers, continues that good work. I would like very much for American readers also to become acquainted with other contemporary poets, remarkable for their unique variety, such as Tvardovsky, Smelyakov, Svetlov, Zabolotsky, Martynov, Slutsky, Vinokurov, Akhmadulina.

Are not the films *The Cranes Are Flying, The Ballad of a Soldier,* the music of Shostakovich and Prokofiev, the performances of Richter, carrying out this sacred duty of art—to unite?

And all that is best in American art also fulfills that duty here in Russia.

I want to say a few words about the role American art has played and still plays in my life.

The first American book I ever read was Harriet Beecher Stowe's *Uncle Tom's Cabin.* I was then some seven years old.

Of course now, no doubt, this book would appear naïve and oversentimental. But at that time it made an extraordinary impression on me. I cried over the fate of Uncle Tom, clenched my fists angrily, ready to hurl myself at the slave driver Simon Legree, and since that time have hated with all my soul that most repulsive thing in the world—slavery—no matter in what civilized form it may appear.

Huckleberry Finn became one of my firmest friends. Tom Sawyer, of course, was also a likeable chap, but you couldn't depend on him as you could on Huck. Huck had a great deal more inner freedom and compassion for the suffering ones, for he himself suffered more than Tom—and he had a great deal more carefree contempt for worldly goods.

Of course in my turn I was a fan of James Fenimore Cooper and Bret Harte, most of whose books I have forgotten now, except the latter's story, *How Santa Claus Came to Simson's Bar*, which still lives in my grateful memory.

The passion of my adolescence was Jack London. There is a great deal I don't care for so much now, but *Martin Eden, The Mexican* and certain other stories still overcome me with their power.

In my youth I swallowed, very unsystematically, Edgar Allan Poe, O'Henry, Dreiser, Sinclair Lewis, Upton Sinclair, Dos Passos, Caldwell. But one book above all other shook me completely. It was *The Grapes of Wrath* by Steinbeck. This book astonished me by its austere bareness and its expression of the highest form of love for man—without emotional priest-like commiseration, without sentimental sighing.

Afterward there were many other works of Steinbeck I liked, in particular *Of Mice and Men, The Winter of Our Discontent, Travels with Charlie*. Nevertheless, the impression from *The Grapes of Wrath* remains unsurpassed. No doubt such a book is written only once in a lifetime.

Later I discovered Hemingway, whose existence was anticipated for me by certain intonations of Stephen Crane—particularly his wonderful story *The Blue Hotel*.

At first I didn't quite grasp Hemingway—he seemed to me too restrained. But afterward I understood that his restraint was the tormented courage of a man, who grits his teeth till the blood runs, in order not to cry out from pain, and still more, who contrives to mock his own pain.

I love many of Hemingway's works, but above all *For Whom the Bell Tolls*. It is said that this book is not very popular in the West. If that is so, I think it only confirms the truism that popularity is a fickle jade. *For Whom the Bell Tolls* is one of the finest books of the twentieth century, which incarnates with truly Shakespearean power the whole *angst* of this century.

I like more than anything, not the famous dialogue in the sleeping bag, but the character of the old woman Pilar, the characters of the partisans and Marty. This novel is terrifying and at the same time piercingly beautiful, like life.

Some people say that the posthumous book of Hemingway, about his youth in Paris, is too caustic, too evil and petty. I don't know—I discovered nothing of this in it. Hemingway is merciless in it, but he was always merciless. But beneath his mercilessness, in this book also, is hidden a wounded love of man.

Cumbersome and unwieldy, Faulkner lurched into my soul, and although thereby it became overcrowded, I still couldn't get him out—couldn't find the strength to move this great mass from the spot. His works are like the formations of a mountain—apparently as irregular and chaotic—but only at first sight. All its promontories, cliffs, chasms, and crags are united into a single mighty whole by some kind of unknown natural power.

Unusually fresh, and original is Salinger's *Catcher in the Rye*, which, incidentally, is beautifully translated into Russian, despite the many difficulties that had to be overcome.

Still later I became acquainted with certain works of Cheever, Farrell, Saroyan, Kerouac, Capote, Updike, Baldwin, and many of them touched me deeply. Of American dramatists known to me, I like most of all the plays of Miller, Williams, and Albee.

A PRECOCIOUS AUTOBIOGRAPHY

A POET'S
AUTOBIOGRAPHY IS HIS POETRY.
Anything else can only be a footnote. A poet is a poet only when
the reader sees him whole, with all his feelings, all his thoughts,
and all his actions, as if the reader held him in the hollow of
his hand.

To be entitled to write with merciless truth about others,
the poet must be mercilessly truthful when he writes about
himself. Splitting the poet's personality in two, into the real
man and the poet, leads inevitably to artistic suicide.

When Arthur Rimbaud became a slave trader, and his life
clashed with the ideals he had held as a poet, he stopped writing
poetry. At least this was an honest way out.

Unfortunately many poets, when their lives clash with their
poetry, continue to write, passing themselves off as different
from what they are.

But they are only deluding themselves when they think they
are writing poetry.

Poetry is not to be deceived.

And poetry deserts those who are false to her.

Poetry is a vindictive woman who never forgives a lie.

Nor will she forgive anything less than the truth. There are
people who pride themselves on never having told a lie in their
whole lives. But let them ask themselves how often they have
failed to tell the truth, preferring a safe silence.

Such people use as an excuse the ancient saying invented by their kind: "Silence is golden."

But if silence is golden, the gold is not pure. This applies to life in general and to poetry in particular, because poetry is life in a concentrated form.

Reticence about oneself in poetry becomes, inevitably, reticence in writing about others—about their sufferings and sorrows.

For a long time many Soviet writers failed to write about their personal thoughts, about their own complexities or conflicts, and, needless to say, about the conflicts and complexities of others. What I have in mind is not only the substitution of the "we" for "I" preached by the Proletcult [1]—the "we" that drummed and thundered from the printed page drowning out the music, subtle and unique, of the individual human personality. Long after the disintegration of the movement, many poems written in the first-person singular still bore the hallmark of that gigantic stage-prop "we." The poet's "I" was purely formal. Even the simple words "I love" were sometimes spoken in so abstract, so oratorical a voice that they might have been "we love."

This was the time when our literary critics came up with the term "lyric hero." According to their recipe, the poet was no longer supposed to be himself in his own poems—he was to turn himself into a symbol.

Outwardly, the poetry of many poets at that time was autobiographical. It contained place names—the poet's native town or village, a list of places he had visited, and some of the events of his life. But in spite of this the poems had no flesh and

[1] Proletarian Culture literary movement.—A.MacA.

blood. Some of the more talented of the writers could be distinguished by their manner of writing. But to tell them apart by their manner of thinking was extremely difficult. It was impossible to feel that they were living, real, existing people because the thoughts and feelings of each individual who really exists are unique and cannot be duplicated.

An autobiography is meaningless if it is only an account of the events in a man's outward life and not also an account of his interior life—of his thoughts and feelings.

What I have said in no way means that I am accusing the whole of Soviet poetry of depersonalizing the author's "I."

When Mayakovsky says "we," he is still Mayakovsky.

Pasternak's "I" is the "I" of Pasternak.

I could easily put down a list of Soviet poets who retained their individuality even through the hardest times, but unfortunately their names would mean nothing to the Western reader.

The work of a true poet is not only a moving, breathing, sound-filled portrait of his time—it is also a self-portrait, just as vivid and just as comprehensive.

Why then, after all I have said about the superfluity of writing memoirs, have I agreed to write an autobiographical sketch? The reason is that many articles that fall into the hands of Western readers represent me as something different from what I am. I am often represented as a colorful figure, startling against the gray background of Soviet society.

This is not what I am at all.

Many Soviet people hate the same things that I hate.

What I am fighting for is just as dear to many of them.

There are people who bring to a society their own original ideas and make that society stronger through these ideas. Theirs is perhaps the highest form of creativity, but I am not of their number.

My poetry is only the expression of moods and ideas already present in Soviet society but which had not so far been expressed in verse. Had I not been there, someone else would have expressed them.

Am I now contradicting what I said before about the poet being, above all, an individual?

Not in the least.

In my opinion, only in a person with a strong, well-defined personality can what is held in common by many be combined and fused.

I should very much like to spend my life expressing the so-far unexpressed ideas of many, while remaining myself. Indeed, if I ceased to be myself, I would not be able to express them.

Who then am I?

I WAS BORN ON JULY 18, 1933, IN SIBERIA, at Zima Junction, a small place near Lake Baikal. My surname, Yevtushenko, is Ukrainian.

Long ago, at the end of the last century, my great-grandfather, a peasant from the Zhitomir Province, was deported to Siberia for having "let out the red rooster" in his landlord's house. This is the Russian peasant way of saying that he had set fire to his house. That's probably the origin of my inclination to reach for that red rooster whenever I meet anyone with a landlord's mentality.

No one in our family uttered the word "Revolution" as if he were making a speech. It was uttered quietly, gently, a shade austerely. Revolution was the religion of our family.

My grandfather, Yermolay Yevtushenko, a soldier who could barely read, was one of the organizers of the peasant movement in the Urals and in eastern Siberia. Later, under the Soviet regime he studied at a military academy, became a brigade commander, and held the important post of deputy commander of artillery in the Russian Republican Army. But even in his commander's uniform he remained the peasant he had always been and kept his religious faith in Revolution.

I last saw him in 1938. I was five then. I remember our conversation very well.

My grandfather came into my room. I had already undressed and was lying in bed. He sat down on the edge of my bed. He had in his hands a box of liqueur-filled chocolates. His eyes, usually mischievous and smiling, that night looked at me from under his gray prickly crew-cut with a tired and sad expression. He offered me the box of chocolates and then pulled a bottle of vodka out of the pocket of his cavalry breeches.

"I want us to have a drink together," he said. "You have the candy and I'll have the vodka."

He slapped the bottom of the bottle with the flat of his hand and the cork shot out. I fished a chocolate out of the box.

"What shall we drink to?" I asked, trying hard to sound grown-up.

"To the Revolution," my grandfather said with grim simplicity.

We touched glasses—that is, my candy touched his bottle—and we drank.

"Now go to sleep," Grandfather said.

He switched off the light but remained sitting on my bed.

It was too dark for me to see his face but I felt that he was looking at me.

Then he began to sing softly. He sang the melancholy songs of the chain gangs, the songs of the strikers and the demonstrators, the songs of the Civil War.

And listening to them I went to sleep. . . .

I never saw my grandfather again. My mother told me he had gone away for a long trip. I didn't know that on that very night he had been arrested on a charge of high treason. I didn't know that my mother stood night after night in that street with the beautiful name, Marine Silence Street, among thousands of other women who were also trying to find out whether their fathers, husbands, brothers, sons were still alive. I was to learn all this later.

Later I also found out what had happened to my other grandfather, who similarly had vanished. He was Rudolph Gangnus, a round-shouldered gray-bearded mathematician of Latvian origin, whose textbooks were used to teach geometry in Soviet schools. He was arrested on a charge of spying for Latvia.

But at this time I knew nothing.

I went with my father and mother to watch the holiday parades, organized workers' demonstrations, and I would beg my father to lift me up a little higher.

I wanted to catch sight of Stalin.

And as I waved my small red flag, riding high in my father's arms above that sea of heads, I had the feeling that Stalin was looking right at me.

I was filled with a terrible envy of those children my age lucky enough to be chosen to hand bouquets of flowers to Stalin and whom he gently patted on the head, smiling his famous smile into his famous mustache.

To explain away the cult of Stalin's personality by saying simply that it was imposed by force is, to say the least, rather naïve. There is no doubt that Stalin exercised a sort of hypnotic charm.

Many genuine Bolsheviks who were arrested at that time utterly refused to believe that this had happened with his knowledge, still less on his personal instructions. Some of them, after being tortured, traced the words "Long live Stalin" in their own blood on the walls of their prison.

Did the Russian people understand what was really happening?

I think the broad masses did not. They sensed intuitively that something was wrong, but no one wanted to believe what he guessed at in his heart. It would have been too terrible.

The Russian people preferred to work rather than to think and to analyze. With a heroic, stubborn self-sacrifice unprecedented in history they built power station after power station, factory after factory. They worked in a furious desperation, drowning with the thunder of machines, tractors, and bulldozers the cries that might have reached them across the barbed wire of Siberian concentration camps.

All the same it was impossible to stop thinking altogether. We were overshadowed by that most dreadful menace in the history of any people—a split between their external and their inner lives.

It was noticeable even to us children. Carefully as our parents shielded us from realizing this discrepancy, their concern only underlined it.

My parents were, psychologically, at opposite poles from one another. This—and not political motives (as was playfully suggested by *Time* magazine)—ultimately led to their divorce.

My father and mother got to know each other at the Geological Institute where both were studying. This was in the twenties.

At that time the great majority of those admitted to the universities were children of workers or peasants. This was a perfectly natural reaction against the Tsarist era when education was reserved for the children of the well-to-do. It was intended to restore the balance. But as so often happens when the balance of justice is restored in too zealous and hot-blooded a way, new injustices were introduced.

In modern Russian this phenomenon is graphically described as "overbending."

Owing to overbending in the system of admissions, the sons and daughters of intellectuals stood out among their fellow students like white crows. This was the case with my father.

One day, at a meeting of the Komsomol (Young Communist League) in his Institute, he was accused of bourgeois leanings just because he happened to wear a tie.

(My father smilingly told me of this incident only the other evening when we couldn't get into a Moscow restaurant because we both were not wearing ties.)

My father's tie did not, however, get in the way of his friendship with the slender girl whose revolutionary principles made her wear a man's red Russian shirt and high boots—this was to be my mother. They soon got married.

My mother, born in Siberia, was not nearly so well read as my father, but to make up for it she had a deep understanding of such things as the land and working with the soil.

I am grateful to my father who when I was a child taught me to love books, and to my mother who gave me in my childhood my love of the soil and of working with my hands. I think that, to the end of my days, I will be half an intellectual and half a peasant. I realize that to be an intellectual is in some ways limiting, but I feel sure that the peasant half of me will always save me from the worst failing of the intellectual—snobbishness.

As I have said, my father was very well read. He was especially fond of history. He would spend hours—though I was still too young to understand him—telling me about the fall of Babylon, the Spanish Inquisition, the Wars of the Roses, and William the Silent. For some reason he was particularly interested in William the Silent. I think he saw in the relationship between him and the mob the embryo of a problem which tormented him at the time—that of the relationship between intellectuals and the Revolution. But I for my part preferred the mob to the Prince of Orange, and to this day my favorite hero is Till Eulenspiegel.

I should very much like to be a Till Eulenspiegel of the atomic age; in his heart, like the ashes of the class society, would rustle the ashes of all who have perished innocently throughout human history—a Till Eulenspiegel who wanders about the earth with his forceful unsophisticated songs, calling upon men to fight for justice. A Till Eulenspiegel who will always loathe inquisitors of whatever sort and laugh at those whose only wish is to fill their belly and to sleep in a soft bed— be they even the nicest of Lamme Goedzaks.[2]

I am grateful to my father who once read Charles de Coster's book to me. My father knew many poems by heart and would recite them for my benefit. He had a prodigious memory. His favorites were Lermontov, Goethe, Poe, and Kipling. He recited Kipling's "If" with the emotion usually kept for the recitation of one's own verse. He did in fact write poetry of his own, and there is no doubt that he was genuinely gifted. A quatrain he wrote when he was fourteen still astonishes me by its exactness:

> *Trying my anguish to hold at bay,*
> *Far away I longed to fly,*
> *But the stars, too high were they,*
> *And the price of them too high.*

Thanks to my father I could read and write by the age of six and, by the time I was eight, I was devouring indiscriminately Dumas, Flaubert, Schiller, Balzac, Dante, Maupassant, Tolstoy, Boccaccio, Shakespeare, Gaidar, Jack London, Cervantes, and Wells. It all made an indescribable salad in my head. I lived in an illusory world, taking not the slightest notice of anything or anyone around me.

I never even noticed that my father and mother were estranged and were only staying together for my sake.

Until June 22, 1941, I was a youthful romantic who thought that people suffered only in books.

[2] A plain and practical Sancho Panza figure in the Till Eulenspiegel legend.—A.MacA.

My first reaction to the war was an aesthetic one—I found it decorative. I loved watching the searchlights fingering the Moscow sky at night. I was gripped with exultation, not with fear, when I heard the howling of the air-raid sirens, and I envied the grownups for being issued such handsome helmets and rifles and sent to a fantastically interesting country called The Front.

But the wounded who came back from that country were somehow rather uncommunicative.

In the autumn of '41, like many other Moscow children, I was evacuated to Siberia.

It took me nearly a month to reach my native Zima Junction, traveling in a train made up of sixteen coaches filled with women and children.

Those sixteen coaches slowly moving deep into the Russian hinterland were heavy with grief and tears.

Coming toward us and heading for the front were flatcars loaded with guns, and boxcars with open doors through which I caught a glimpse of the young freckled faces of soldiers. But by then I was no longer charmed by their rifles and helmets. Nor did I believe that they felt gay and happy, even when the stirring tunes they whistled or played on their accordions reached me from the boxcars. I no longer felt that suffering was something confined to books.

And when I came to Zima Junction I witnessed what perhaps was the most terrible thing I have seen in my life—the weddings of 1941.

Young boys called up to the front were handed their papers and given two or three days to get ready. The times were grim.

The German general Guderian was looking Moscow over through his field glasses. These young men, whose bodies were to block his way to Moscow, had hardly any chance of coming back. Many of them were engaged. Their girls chose to be their wives if only for a day and at the cost of being widowed at once. These were the terrible weddings I saw, weddings where the first night of married life was to be the last.

I used to be good at folk dancing, and at the age of eight I was taken to these weddings to dance and was paid for my performance with a piece of bread or a potato. But all this I have described in my poem "Weddings."

When today I think about war and what it means, it is these weddings that come to my mind first. And this memory affects me much more than all the fine speeches about the need to fight for peace.

The word "peace" can have a concrete meaning only for those who know what war is. If it were possible to be grateful to a war, I would thank the War for giving me an understanding of the word "peace." And I would also like to thank the War for helping me to understand the words "my country."

I began to realize that "my country" was not a geographical or literary concept—it referred to living people. I despise nationalism. For me the world contains only two nations: the nation of good people and the nation of bad people. I am a nationalist of the nation of good people.

But the love of mankind can only be reached through the love of one's country.

Does this mean that it was only through patriotism that Russia was victorious in the war?

No, that isn't the whole story.

As I have said earlier, before the war the Russian people were overshadowed by the danger of living a split life.

Nevertheless, in the bottom of their hearts and in spite of everything—even in spite of all the horrors of Stalin's concentration camps—the Russian people never lost faith in the ideals of the Revolution. And when the war broke out they rose to defend not only their country but also their Revolution. It is no mere coincidence that the poet Mikhail Kulchitsky, who was killed in action at the age of twenty, wrote:

> *And once again, through the blue mists*
> *Secret convoys are rolling in,*
> *And communism is close again*
> *As it was in nineteen-nineteen.*

Hard as it is to admit, the war lightened the Russians' spiritual burden, for they no longer needed to be insincere. And this was one of the chief causes of our victory.

All of us, from the smallest to the greatest, whether soldiers or workers, peasants or intellectuals, gave everything to the war effort—and I too tried to be a part of it. I helped with the harvest, worked in a sawmill, gathered medicinal herbs for the wounded.

That was when I began to write, at first in prose.

It was difficult to get paper at that time. A thin notebook cost as much as two pounds of butter. At school we did our spelling exercises on old newspapers, writing between the lines of the war communiqués. I had decided to write a novel. So I swiped my grandmother's two-volume edition of Marx and Engels, and in the course of a year filled in all the spaces between the lines.

My grandmother forgave me. She patted me on the head and said: "Well, that ought to make you a convinced Marxist."

I believe my grandmother's prediction was correct.

I WAS NOT YET WRITING VERSE BUT I PUT DOWN

all the folk songs and ballads I heard in the villages—not with any utilitarian purpose but as though I were instinctively afraid that many of the treasures of folk language would vanish from human memory. It was through the folk sayings and proverbs I heard, always full of metaphors and aphorisms, that the many-faceted beauty of the Russian language was revealed to me.

There in the Siberian countryside, as though sheltered by the taiga from the pollution of the cities, the Russian language remained pure. Language is like snow—always covered with soot from factory chimneys in the cities and only in the country virginally fresh.

The songs and ballads I collected had the very smell of the taiga.

Almost unconsciously I slipped into the habit of writing verses of my own, in the mode of folklore.

I wanted them to smell of the taiga too.

People have often asked me who taught me to write poetry. My first teacher was the taiga.

I loved her for her severity and her inherent pride. To those who came to her against their wishes, the taiga looked grim and bleak. But to those who came to her with an open heart, she was always kind and, in a way, shyly tender.

It seemed to me a terrible sacrilege to hurt the taiga, if only by breaking off the smallest twig without good reason.

And although I am not a vegetarian, I still thought it criminal to destroy the many beasts and birds of the taiga, who have never done any harm to man.

One winter night my uncles came home from the taiga. They drank noisily all night through, their husky voices singing songs as slow, meandering, and never-ending as Russian rivers. Finally they put out the lights and went to bed.

I went out onto the porch in my pants and slippers for a drink of water, and stumbled against something. It gave off a strange booming sound. I fumbled in the darkness for a box of matches and by their uncertain light saw, piled one upon another, the frozen bodies of several roe deer. The forty-below temperature had made them so hard they resounded when struck. Their legs pointed at the roof. Their large eyes gazed at me questioningly, as if they were human. As though hypnotized, I sank down on my bare knees on the rime-covered floor. I pressed their icy bodies close to me and tried to move them. I tried breathing on them. At first I thought they were only frozen. Then I noticed that one of them had a tiny spot of blood on its delicate, childlike forehead.

I flung my arms around the animal and burst into bitter sobs.

My uncles woke up and came rushing out. They had to struggle to pull me away from the deer, and were quite unable to understand why it took me so long afterward to calm down.

It was indeed hard to understand why any boy should weep

over the bodies of roe deer at a time when so much human blood was being shed.

I myself, when I heard the news from the front over the radio, rejoiced at the number of Germans who had been killed, though I also wept over the deer.

I could not see the Germans as human beings.

They were the Enemy.

In '44 my mother took me back to Moscow. There I saw the Enemy for the first time. If my memory is right, nearly 20,000 German prisoners of war were to be marched in a single column through the streets of Moscow.

The pavements swarmed with onlookers, cordoned off by soldiers and police.

The crowd was made up mostly of women—Russian women, with hands chapped and roughened by hard work, lips untouched by lipstick and thin hunched shoulders which had borne half the burden of the war. Every one of them must have had a father or a husband, a brother or a son killed by the Germans.

Full of hatred, the women gazed in the direction from which the column of prisoners was about to appear.

At last we saw it.

The Nazi generals were marching at the head, their massive chins stuck arrogantly out, the corners of their lips scornfully turned down. Their whole demeanor was meant to show their superiority over their plebeian conquerors.

"The bastards stink of perfume," a woman in the crowd spat with hatred.

The women's work-worn hands were clenched into fists. The

soldiers and policemen had all they could do to hold them back.

Then suddenly something happened to these women.

They saw the simple German soldiers, thin, unshaven, covered with dirty bloodstained bandages, hobbling on crutches or leaning on the shoulders of their comrades. And the soldiers walked with their heads down.

The street became dead silent—the only sound was the shuffling of boots and the thumping of crutches.

The soldiers were no longer enemies.

They were people.

IN 1944 I
WAS LIVING ALONE IN AN EMPTY
apartment in a small quiet Moscow street, Chetvertaya Meshchanskaya.

My parents were divorced. My father was somewhere in Kazakhstan with his new wife and their two children. I seldom received letters from him.

My mother was at the front. She had given up her work as a geologist to become a singer and was giving concerts for the troops.

My education was left to the street. The street taught me to swear, smoke, spit elegantly through my teeth, and to keep my fists up, always ready for a fight—a habit which I have kept to this day.

The street taught me not to be afraid of anything or anyone—this is another habit I have kept.

I realized that what mattered in the struggle for existence was to overcome my fear of those who were stronger.

The ruler of our street, Chetvertaya Meshchanskaya, was a boy of about sixteen who was nicknamed Red.

Red's shoulders were incredibly broad for a boy of his age.

Red walked masterfully up and down our street, his legs wide apart and with a slightly rolling gait, like a seaman on the deck of his ship.

From under his peaked cap, always worn back to front, his forelock tumbled down in a fiery cascade, and out of his round pockmarked face, green eyes, like a cat's, sparkled with scorn for everything and everyone crossing his path. Two or three lieutenants, in peaked caps back to front like Red's, trotted at his heels.

Red could stop any boy and say impressively the one word "money." His lieutenants would turn out the boy's pockets, and if he resisted they gave him a real beating.

Everyone was afraid of Red. I too was afraid. I knew he carried heavy brass knuckles in his pocket.

I wanted to conquer my fear of Red.

So I wrote a poem about him.

This was my first piece of journalism in verse.

By the next day the whole street knew the piece by heart and relished it with triumphant hatred.

One morning on my way to school I suddenly came upon Red and his lieutenants. His eyes seemed to bore through me. "Ah, the poet," he drawled, smiling crookedly. "So you write verses. Do they rhyme?"

Red's hand darted into his pocket and came out armed with its brass knuckles; it flashed like lightning and struck my head. I fell down streaming with blood and lost consciousness.

This was my first payment as a poet.

I spent several days in bed.

When I went out, with my head still bandaged, I again saw Red. I struggled with instinctive fear but lost and took to my heels.

I ran all the way home. There I rolled on my bed, biting my pillow and pounding it with my fists in shame and impotent fury at my cowardice.

But then I made up my mind to vanquish it at whatever cost.

I went into training with parallel bars and weights, and after every session I would feel my muscles. They were getting harder, but slowly. Then I remembered something I had read in a book about a miraculous Japanese method of wrestling which gave an advantage to the weak over the strong. I sacrificed a week's ration card for a textbook on jujitsu.

For three weeks I hardly left home—I trained with two other boys. Finally I felt I was ready and went out.

Red was sitting on the lawn in our yard, playing Twenty-one with his lieutenants. He was absorbed in the game.

Fear was still in me and it ordered me to turn back. But I went up to the players and kicked the cards aside with my foot.

Red looked up, surprised at my impudence after my recent flight.

He got up slowly. "You looking for more?" he asked menacingly.

As before, his hand dived into his pocket for the brass knuckles. But I made a quick jabbing movement, and Red, howling with pain, rolled on the ground. Bewildered, he got up and came at me, swinging his head furiously from side to side like a bull.

I caught his wrist and squeezed slowly, as I had read in the book, until the brass knuckles dropped from his limp fingers. Nursing his hand, Red fell down again. He was sobbing and smearing the tears over his pockmarked face with his grimy fist. His lieutenants discreetly withdrew.

That day Red ceased to rule our street.

And from that day on I knew for certain that there is no need to fear the strong. All one needs is to know the method of overcoming them. There is a special jujitsu for every strong man.

What I also learned that day was that, if I wished to be a poet, I must not only write poems but also know how to stand up for what I have written.

MY MOTHER CAME HOME FROM THE FRONT.

She looked strange—very thin and her hair was black; it had been fair.

At first I thought she had dyed it. I asked her about it.

My mother smiled sadly and took off her wig. Underneath it

her cropped hair stood up on end like a boy's. She had caught typhus and at the military hospital they had shaved her head. Something had happened to her voice. At the front she had given several concerts a day, standing on a truck or a tank, singing to men who were going off to die.

She told me they were her most appreciative listeners.

She had sung to them in rain or blizzard, with no means of getting warm except now and then a gulp of vodka from some soldier's flask.

Her voice, which had been beautiful and strong, began to give way. It cracked under the strain.

When she came back my mother found a job, but she didn't tell me where.

One day some boys in my class asked me: "Is your mother a singer?"

"Yes," I said proudly.

"Where does she sing?"

"I don't know. At some theater, I suppose."

"Some theater!" They laughed derisively. "She's singing at a movie house—the Forum!"

THE DAY OF VICTORY OVER GERMANY ARRIVED.
Rocket after rocket splashed into the sky, and little boys ran along the streets trying to catch the dazzling drops.

Disabled soldiers who sold cigarettes were giving them away free.

Some general had bought a whole ice-cream cart and was offering the contents to the children.

People were hugging each other, crying and laughing. It seemed to them that all their troubles were over and a wonderfully cloudless life would now begin.

As for me, I went to the Forum movie house.

The foyer, packed with soldiers and women, smelled of beer and cheap perfume. Vodka bottles, which the audience had brought with them, passed from hand to hand. People swallowed straight from the bottle and kissed greedily between swigs. The attendants closed their eyes to both vodka and kissing —everything was allowed that day.

No one took the slightest notice of the little orchestra playing martial music on a tiny stage.

I shuddered as a woman came on in a dress covered with sequins, in golden shoes and with a thick black mop of hair which, I already knew, concealed a timid, boyish crew-cut. It was my mother. She came up to the microphone and began to sing. Her voice quavered and only now and then was it possible to guess at its former beauty.

No one listened to her.

They preferred to kiss and drink, drink and kiss. Damn it, it was Victory Day! And for that victory twenty million Russians had given their lives, and my mother—her voice.

Afterward she and I walked home through the Moscow streets by night, through the shouting, the laughter, and the music. I was carrying her suitcase. Packed inside it were her sequined dress and her golden shoes. Her feet were once again in army boots.

"I was awful, wasn't I?" she asked me.

"Of course not. How can you say such a thing! You were very good," I answered hastily.

She gave me a long look and sadly patted me on the head.

Soon after this Mother gave up the stage and took a run-of-the-mill job in theater management. It was tense, exhausting work and brought in very little money—700 rubles a month. On this salary my mother, making many sacrifices, brought us up—my sister Yelena, born during the war, and myself.

I gave my mother a lot of trouble.

I had an impossible character. My avid curiosity about life kept getting me into the most incredible situations.

Once I got mixed up with professional thieves and another time with people who dealt in the black market in books.

It was always my mother who came to my rescue.

My mother, like Lenin, preached work, work, and more work.

But as it happened, my schoolwork was remarkably bad.

There were subjects I couldn't cope with at all—physics for instance. Incidentally I still can't make out what electricity is or where it comes from. And I always got bad marks for my grammar and syntax lessons. I made hardly any mistakes in writing and I could see no point in sweating at rules when I could write correctly without them.

The distinguishing features of people of my generation were already noticeable at school, though of course only in an embryonic form. There on the school benches sat the future seekers after truth, the future heroes, the future cynics, and the future dogmatists.

I already disliked idle cynics who mocked at everything and everyone, just as I could not abide those model pupils who worked hard but without using their brains and accepted everything they were told without question.

Sitting at my desk under the portrait of Stalin, I gazed avidly through the window at the world outside, where snowflakes somersaulted slowly in the air. And when school was over I liked to escape to my other school—the noisy school of the big city smelling of snow, cigarettes, gasoline, and hot cabbage pies sold by red-cheeked women standing in the frost.

When I came home, I sat down at my desk, spread my notebooks neatly around me, and as soon as Mama, pleased that I should be doing my homework, left the room, I wrote poetry. In those poems I tried to invent a different life for myself. I stopped only when my hand felt completely numb. Sometimes I wrote ten or twelve poems in one day. I bombarded editors with my verses and unfailingly received them back with a rejection slip. I can just imagine what the editors of *Pioneer Truth* [3] thought of a schoolboy's verses such as these:

> Headlong I rushed along my never-ending way
> Frightening away night's shadow.
> You loved me, women met by chance,
> Only to'forget me on the morrow.

Once I copied out all my poems in a fat notebook and sent it to the editorial office of *Young Guard*.

For the first time I got a letter back asking me to come in. It was signed by the poet Andrey Dostal. I went to see him.

[3] *Pionerskaya pravda*—organ of the Pioneers, an organization similar to the Cub Scouts but under Party control.—A.MacA.

Andrey Dostal, a spare young man with a patch over one eye which made him look like a pirate, asked me in surprise: "Hello, boy, whom did you want to speak to?"

I showed him his letter.

"I suppose your father couldn't come? I hope he's not ill."

"It was I who wrote to you, not my father," I snapped, nervously clutching my schoolbag.

Dostal gave me a bewildered look and burst out laughing.

"Well, you certainly fooled me there. I was expecting a gray-beard, somebody who's been through fire and water. Just look at your poems—there's war and sorrows and the tragedies of love. . . ."

There were other people in the room who were also looking at me and smiling.

I thought they were making fun of me and my eyes began to fill with tears.

But Dostal, realizing this, put his arm around my shoulders, made me sit next to him, and spoke to me about the fat notebook I had sent him. Later on we became friends. He was not a great poet but he loved poetry and he wanted to see me accomplish what he had failed to achieve himself. In general, in everything to do with my writing, it was the lesser poets who helped me. They are often kinder and take more trouble than the "great." All the same my poems were once again turned down.

However, I kept *Martin Eden* permanently on my desk and its first pages were an inspiration and a help to me. At that time, it was the opening pages that seemed to me the point of Jack London's book. Now I like the end best.

But I am running ahead.

My mother didn't want me to become a poet.

Not because she didn't like poetry—she did—but because she was convinced of one thing: a poet was an unsettled, insecure, restless, tormented creature. The fate of almost every Russian poet had been tragic. Pushkin and Lermontov were both killed in duels; Blok, burning himself out, virtually committed suicide; Yesenin hanged himself; Mayakovsky shot himself. And although she never spoke of this to me, she must have known of the many poets who had died in Stalin's camps. All this made her worry about my future, tear up my notebooks, and urge me to take up something, as she put it, "more serious."

But it was poetry that seemed to me the most serious thing in the world.

And I continued to write with the obstinacy of a youthful maniac.

Needless to say, I wasn't visited by any profound thoughts, but I was concerned with poetic form.

Thus for several years I worked at rhymes.

The system of rhyming used in contemporary poems seemed to me limiting.

Back in the 1920's Mayakovsky had written:

> *Surely,*
> *a dozen,*
> *as yet unused rhymes*
> *Survive,*
> *somewhere in Venezuela.*

But I did not believe Mayakovsky, though I was very fond of him, for he had himself taught that in literature one should not be too impressed by established authorities. I didn't take the easy way out adopted by many Western poets who look on rhyme as altogether obsolete and write something between poetry and prose, thereby murdering a precious quality in poetry —its music.

For several years I sat down every evening with an enormous Russian dictionary and, going through it in alphabetical order, searched for new rhymes that had never yet been used in poetry.

In the end I had a notebook with something like 10,000 new rhymes, which unfortunately vanished. But in this way a new system of rhyming was worked out, which afterward was known by my name. The attribution was not exact, for I discovered nothing new but only elaborated a principle of rhyming which occurs in Russian folklore. Unfortunately it is hard for me to explain it to the Western reader because the point gets completely lost in translation.

While I was trying to write better and better poetry, my schoolwork got worse and worse.

"This isn't going to get you either money or a peaceful life," said my mother, tearing up my current notebook.

But I hated the very thought of a peaceful life.

And I despised money.

Some eminent person once said that money is the means to freedom.

But as I understand it, money always was and still is the means of making people into slaves.

Its absence too is slavery because people need it in order to exist.

And it makes slaves of those who have it and spend their nerves and their energy on getting more of it or at least keeping what they have.

I witnessed the currency reform of 1947.[4] When the rumor spread that it was imminent, people mobbed the stores and bought up everything. . . . I saw a man loading four toilet seats on a car because the hardware store had nothing else left. I saw a woman staggering, sweating and puffing, under the weight of a plaster Venus. The day the reform was officially announced, I saw an old man running down the street, screaming in hysterics as he scattered handfuls of money on the ground and trampled on them.

With my frozen hands stuck into the pockets of an old, patched woman's overcoat, I watched these people with a revolutionary's scornful gaze.

I liked going to the movies and seeing films about the Revolution. A lump came into my throat when soldiers and workers with red armbands and rifles in their hands moved across the screen. I wanted to be like them—to be as proud and as unselfish.

It was strange and unaccountable to me that even people with Party cards in their pockets could love money so much.

To me "Communist" and "disinterested" meant the same thing.

I remember the father of one of my school friends, a man high up in a trade organization, pompously quoting Lenin's words: "Under communism we will use gold to build latrines." The quotation delighted me. But on the day of the currency reform, my friend's father was found dead. He had shot himself and lay beside a gutted mattress stuffed with devalued rubles.

Gradually it dawned on me that many people who called

[4] The new 1947 ruble was fixed at ten old rubles.—A.MacA.

themselves Communists and eagerly quoted Lenin and Stalin at every opportunity were in reality not Communists at all.

For these people, having Party membership cards in their pockets and talking about communism were simply ways of getting ahead and had nothing to do with their ideological convictions.

Later on, I wrote about such people in a poem, "Consider Me a Communist":

> *All those who fuss,*
> *at meetings, and fret,*
> *Pouring out lies in a shower,*
> *Don't care*
> *that the power is*
> *Soviet.*
> *All they care*
> *is that it is power.*

As a child I could not of course define all this; I only felt much of it intuitively.

But the romantic ideals of the workers and soldiers who stormed the Winter Palace in 1917 are as precious to me now as when I was a child, while those who are preoccupied with personal gain will always be traitors to the Revolution in my eyes.

The first mistake made by Western students of the Russian Revolution is to judge the revolutionary idea not by those who are genuinely loyal to it, but by those who betray it.

Their other mistake is that they still regard the idea of communism as something imposed by force on the Russian people, without realizing that by now it is a part of the Russian people's flesh and blood.

"Russia," Lenin once said, "has paid for Marxism with her suffering." What he had in mind was the Tsarist past. But it was not only with her suffering under the Tsars that Russia paid the price of Marxism; she also paid it with the errors made and the torments she endured in the course of building a socialist society.

I love my fellow countrymen not only as a Russian but also as a revolutionary. I love them all the more because in spite of everything they have never become cynical, they have never lost their faith in the original purity of the revolutionary idea in spite of all the filth that has since desecrated it.

I hate the cynics with their lordly view of history, their scorn for the heroic labors of my countrymen, whom they try to represent as a lost flock of sheep, their skill for lumping the good with the bad and spitting at the whole thing, and their utter inability to offer any constructive alternative.

But dogmatism, which I regard as revisionism in one of its most horrible forms, is just as hateful to me. . . .

It is true that dogmatism can be unselfishly fanatical, but much more often—as I have realized ever since my childhood—it serves as a cloak for selfish vested interests.

One should not confuse ideas with the unworthy men who use them as weapons in their personal struggle for survival.

And since, as I have said, communism has become the very essence of the Russian people, it follows that both cynics and dogmatists are not only traitors to the Revolution, but traitors to their own people as well.

Throughout the many centuries of their history, the Russians have suffered perhaps more than any other people on earth.

It might be thought that suffering degrades and blunts the

human spirit, destroying its capacity to believe in anything. Yet if we look closely at the history of the nations, we see that the opposite is true.

It is the more fortunate nations, those favored by their geographical position and historical circumstances, that today show a grosser spirit and a weaker hold on moral principles.

Nor would I call these nations happy in spite of all the outward signs of their prosperity.

Never has the ancient biblical saying—man does not live by bread alone—had such a convincing ring of truth as it does today.

Some great thinker once said that man is an animal with a capacity for dreaming. There are men whose lives confirm only the first part of this proposition. Yet if we look into their hearts we find that, although they have no lofty dreams, there are dreams nevertheless, for man has a need to dream.

However prosperous, a man will always be dissatisfied if he has no high ideal. And whatever devices he may use to conceal his dissatisfaction even from himself, these will only make him feel more dissatisfied.

But if even the rich feel burdened by the lack of an ideal, to those who suffer real deprivation an ideal is a first necessity of life. Where there is plenty of bread and a shortage of ideals, bread is no substitute for an ideal. But where bread is short ideals are bread.

Such is human nature. Man is an idealist by nature, and only great sufferings give birth to great ideals.

Why was Marx mistaken when he predicted that the Revolution would occur first in the country with the most advanced industrial development? How did it happen that, in spite of his prophecies, the first country to adopt the revolutionary path of socialism was Russia, industrially so backward?

The answer is that this country, so lagging in terms of industrial development, was perhaps the most advanced in terms of her people's sorrows and tears.

"Yes," you may say, "but side by side with its triumphs the Revolution brought the Russian people new sorrows and new tears." And that is true.

But here our special Russian character must be kept in mind. Suffering is a sort of habit with us. What seems nearly unendurable to others we endure more easily.

Besides, we have paid for our ideal with so much blood and torment that the cost itself has endeared it and made it more precious to us, as a child born in pain is more precious to its mother.

You may say: "But doesn't it occur to you that communism itself may be a false ideal?"

If the reader believes in God I will ask him: "Can you equate the substance of the Christian religion with the swindlers who used to make a handsome profit by selling indulgences, with the Inquisitors, the priests who got rich at their parishioners' expense, or parishioners who pray piously in church and lie and cheat outside its walls?"

Neither can I, a believing Communist, equate the essence of my religion with the crooks who climb on its bandwagon, with its inquisitors, its crafty, avaricious priests, or its double-dealing, two-faced parishioners.

My feeling about these things comes from way back, from my childhood.

"Call him a Communist!" my mother would say about some

liar, yesman, some careerist or pompous bureaucrat who used his Party card to help him climb the social ladder.

And to this day, for me a Communist is not merely someone who belongs to the organization and pays his dues. A Communist is a man who puts the people's interests above his own, but who, at the same time, would never wantonly squander human lives in the name of those interests.

I am ashamed for Stalin, though not only for him. How was it possible for him so to distrust the people? For the people showed such a boundless faith in communism and extended that faith to Stalin and those around him.

All right, we'll stop talking about 1937 if you like. But the people who fought so heroically after all they had endured that year, and who then so heroically rebuilt their country from its ruins and ashes, did they deserve his distrust?

The war was over, but many of those who brought about the victory were again under suspicion and surveillance, if not actually arrested. I of course had no idea of the scale on which this was being done, but I saw a good deal, and what I sensed without consciously grasping it found an outlet in my rebellion against school.

At school I fought the squealers, the yesmen, the teachers' pets.

I soon earned the reputation of a hoodlum. When I reached the eleventh grade, I was moved to a new school, a dumping ground for the hopeless cases whom other Moscow schools were anxious to get off their hands. I didn't stay there long, for even in that environment my rebelliousness stood out.

One day someone broke into the principal's office and stole all the class records and report cards.

A general meeting was called.

For six hours the principal argued, pleaded, and threatened in the hope of discovering the name of the culprit. But no one confessed.

Finally, enraged, he pointed a plump, accusing finger at me. "It was you."

I got up and said he was mistaken.

"You! It was you! You did it!" the principal shouted.

I realized it would be useless for me to argue.

The next day I was expelled.

Seven years later, when I was beginning to be known as a poet, I found out the truth—at a class reunion dinner I attended.

It was natural to suspect me because my work was so bad that I'd got an F in German on the very day of the theft.

But at this reunion a young man came up to me, who had been one of the few all-round brilliant students at our school and had always had top grades in every subject.

With an embarrassed smile he said to me: "You know, it was I who stole the class records."

It turned out that he had been resentful at getting slightly less than a top grade that day.

It occurred to me with some bitterness that this was typical of life. How often are crimes committed by those who are models of propriety? No one dreams of suspecting them and the blame is taken by those, usually innocent, who stay at the bottom of the class and have the reputation for being hoodlums.

For some time after I was expelled I tried to keep it a secret from my mother who, I knew, would be very much upset, but she soon found out. She cried and begged me to go to the principal and ask him to forgive me, and she wanted to see someone herself. But I had my pride.

I quarreled with Mother and ran away to join my father. I traveled on the roof of a train all the way to Kazakhstan.

I was fifteen.

I wanted to become a man and stand on my own feet. At that time my father was working as chief of a geological expedition.

When I arrived, ragged and skinny, he looked me over and said: "So you want to stand on your own feet. . . . Well, if you really do, no one here must know you're my son. Otherwise you'll be favored whether you want it or not, and that isn't going to make a man of you."

I joined the expedition as a laborer.

I learned to break the ground with a pick, split off samples of rock as flat as my hand with a mallet, to use a razor blade to make three matches out of the only one we had left, and to light a fire in driving rain.

I COULDN'T SWIM. AND I LIVED IN FEAR
of being found out and disgraced.

One day I was walking with a geologist along a narrow mountain path above a noisy stream. We both carried knapsacks filled with specimens of rock. Suddenly the geologist took a false step and the ground gave way under his feet. He tried to catch hold of a bush, missed it, and fell headlong from the steep bank, down into the river. Within seconds I saw him thrashing about in the foaming water, struggling to keep afloat, but his knapsack was dragging him down.

I flung mine off my shoulders, whipped my knife from inside my belt, and jumped in.

It was not till I had swum up to the geologist, cut the straps of his knapsack, and we had both scrambled ashore that I remembered I didn't know how to swim.

And from that day on I have known that the best way of learning something is to take a leap into the unknown without looking back. That way, you either learn or perish.

I learned not to be squeamish.

We had a Kazakh cook with us.

One of his daily duties was to harness an old horse to a cart with a wooden barrel and fetch water from a stream four or five miles away from our tents. In this water he cooked our tinned soup and cereal; it was the water we drank and the water we used to wash ourselves and our shirts.

Every day we went off as the sun was rising and stayed out till sunset. All day long we wandered over the parched Kazakh steppe under the molten sun, looking for minerals, and by evening we were bent double by the weight of our knapsacks. I remember that at first my back, cut by the sharp edges of the rock samples, had open sores on it—they later hardened into calluses. But we kept on until our sacks were full. However, one day we gave up and decided to start for camp earlier than usual.

The sun blazed mercilessly.

Our canteens were empty and our lips parched.

We were walking back, our minds filled with vivid images of the deep, long gulps of water we would drink on our return, scooping it out of the barrel with a pitcher.

Suddenly we heard the sound of a strange song coming from beyond a hill. We exchanged puzzled looks and quickened our pace. Coming around the hill, we saw our horse slowly pulling the cart with the water barrel. No one seemed to be driving and no human being was in sight. Where could the song be coming from?

The sound was growing louder and louder.

Suddenly we saw the cook's head sticking out of the barrel. Up to his neck in cool water, with the hundred-degree heat outside, he was splashing about like a baby in a tub, thoroughly enjoying himself. And flooded with *joie de vivre*, he was singing in his guttural voice a song of joy and triumph.

We wasted no words. With grim determination we set off at a run for the barrel.

The cook saw us and closed his eyes in horror.

We pulled him out of the barrel and he stood before us in all his primordial beauty.

We didn't hit him. We only shook him by the shoulders and asked him: "Have you been doing this all the time, you bastard, or is this the first time?"

"It's the first time! It's the first time!" he cried, his teeth chattering with terror.

We let him go and looked at the water, torn between thirst and revulsion.

The river was far away and we lacked the strength for another journey.

At last one of us said grimly: "Hell, it's still water," and dipped his canteen into the barrel.

He tipped it up and drank greedily. I drank that water too. Life was knocking the city squeamishness out of me.

BUT THE SAME HARD GRIM LIFE WAS TEACHING

me to have a new faith in human beings.

One day I discovered I had lice. My clothes were crawling with the filthy vermin. I was in despair; I didn't know what to do.

I ran off into the steppe and climbed down into an abandoned hole. There I took off all my clothes and set about killing the lice. Somewhere high above me the grass rustled, the birds sang, and the clouds rolled through the sky, while there I stood, hating myself, naked, alone, shivering with cold and disgust, at the bottom of my pit with the frogs giving me scornful looks.

I simply couldn't put on other clothes because I had no others.

Suddenly it grew darker in the pit and, looking up through the rectangular opening, I saw a young peasant woman, barefooted and with a yoke slung over her shoulders, standing at the edge.

I pressed myself hard against the side of the pit, wishing I could vanish into the earth and, sobbing with shame, covered my face with my hands.

There was a soft thump as the woman jumped down.

She pulled my hands away from my face. From between long black lashes intensely blue eyes looked at me with a warm concern which is much better than pity.

"What are you crying for?" asked the woman. "Come along with me."

I pulled on my clothes somehow and, hanging my head in confusion, followed her.

She lit the stove in her bathhouse, scrubbed me like a small child, steamed my clothes, and put me to bed.

That night as I lay on a wooden trestle-bed under a sheep-skin coat, she came and sat on the edge of the bed. She had only her nightgown on.

"Do you feel better now, you silly child? How could you get in such a state? . . . You mustn't be afraid of people—people will always help you if you're in trouble."

She stroked my hair.

I drew back and again burst into tears. I was so disgusted with myself, I was sure I disgusted everyone else.

"What a fuss. . . . I suppose you've got it into your head that you're disgusting. You're not in the least."

She lay down next to me under the sheepskin, her big strong body with its clean, bathhouse smell of birch leaves pressed against mine.

I shall never forget her.

That day I found out that all values in this world are more or less questionable, but that the most important thing in life is human kindness.

The kindness of a woman is a beautiful and unique thing.

It is true that every woman is above all a mother, and when she strokes our hair, it's as if we were her children and her touch has something motherly in it.

I ALSO KNEW ANOTHER SORT OF HUMAN WARMTH, rougher and more self-conscious—the fatherly kindness of men.

There were the soldiers, during the war, who clumsily pushed into my hand lumps of sugar stuck with shreds of tobacco; the peasants who once rescued me from an angry she-bear in the taiga; the geologists who refused to let me carry my knapsack when it was too heavy and shifted it to their own shoulders; the workmen who cured the torn bleeding blisters on my feet with herbs—ever since my childhood all these people have built up my faith in the human race and in the greatest human quality—kindness.

All of us when we are starting out in life have our special demons who try to kill our faith in human beings, to make us doubt the very possibility of an unselfish motive in anyone, demons with smooth, enticing hands who try to lure us forever into dark labyrinths of cynical distrust.

And when I was young, I too had such a demon.

My demon worked as an engineer in one of the mines in

Kazakhstan. He was about forty-five, with a big bald head set on a squat body, and with tiny, mocking eyes.

The demon would ask me out in the evening, after work, and sit holding forth on such themes as: all men are scoundrels; or, love and friendship and all other such altruistic notions have been invented by novelists who, like the rest of us, are bastards in their private lives.

The demon had a woman living with him—a plain, thin, sad-looking little woman with the evasive eyes of a beaten dog. She had once been a dishwasher in the miners' messhall.

He used her as a sitting target for his contempt. Every evening when he came home she had to wash his feet, and he especially enjoyed this ritual if there happened to be someone around. He clearly felt that it exalted him while degrading the rest of mankind in the person of this uncomplaining woman.

One night when he was talking to me he ordered her to bring a basin into which he lowered his feet. He sat wriggling his hairy toes in the warm water with delight.

The demon was philosophizing:

"You believe that what keeps society together is love, don't you? Well, take this woman and myself. I sleep with her though I despise her, and she hates me but sleeps with me, and, what's more, washes my feet every night. Why do we stay together? Because we need each other. I need her to sleep with and to wash my feet. And she needs me to feed and clothe her. Society is not based on love but on mutual hatred."

I looked at the woman.

She continued to wash her tormentor's feet, her tears rolling down her cheeks and falling into the dirty, soapy water, next to the blissfully wiggling toes.

The demon's arguments were abhorrent yet convincing. All the same, the more they seemed to be supported by facts, the stronger grew my resistance to them.

One day the demon took me by truck to fetch the workmen's pay from a small town across the steppe. Our driver was a taciturn young man with a solid row of steel teeth and tattooed hands.

"Keep an eye on him, he's done time," the demon whispered to me before we set out. "We'll have quite a lot of money on us. I've got something here—" He patted the pocket in which he kept his revolver. "Still, you'd better keep an eye on him."

We called at the bank. The demon carefully counted the packets of creased rubles and put them away in a worn leather brief case. Then we all three got back into the cab of the truck —the driver, the demon with the brief case on his knees, and I.

Before us lay a journey of close to three hundred miles through almost trackless desert.

All we could see around us were the dead glimmer of salt lakes and the steppe eagles perched on telegraph poles, majestically turning their tiny heads toward us.

When we were halfway home the demon resumed his philosophizing:

"Isn't life fascinating?" he addressed the driver. "I know that you know that there's money in my brief case which you wouldn't mind taking for yourself. But you also know that I have a revolver in my pocket, and that in any case you couldn't get away with it even if you killed me. . . . But otherwise you'd kill me, wouldn't you?"

The demon chuckled, pleased with himself.

The driver said nothing, but his tattooed hands tightened on the wheel.

"All men are by nature thieves and murderers," the demon went on. "But they're afraid of being punished. Take away the penalties and everyone would steal and kill."

Suddenly the driver jammed his foot on the brake.

I hit the windshield with my head, and when a moment later I recovered from the shock, the revolver was in the driver's hand and pointing at the demon's stomach.

"Get out, you bastard," the driver said tonelessly. "Every time you open your mouth, toads come hopping out. It stinks too much like a swamp with you in here. Get out and leave the money behind!" He snatched the brief case from the demon's shaking hand, pushed him out, and stepped on the accelerator. We drove on.

"You know what he's thinking about me now?" snorted the driver. "He thinks I'm going to make off with the money. These crooks think everybody's like themselves. Give them half a chance and they'll foul up the whole world and we'll all be wading knee-deep in shit."

I looked back. In the distance in the middle of the empty steppe a small demon was shouting inaudibly and grotesquely waving his arms as he ran after us, but he was growing smaller and smaller.

"You needn't worry about him," the driver grunted. "He won't get lost. That kind always falls on their feet—unfortunately."

We drove on.

After a while the truck stopped.

"Water's gone—boiled away," said the driver gruffly after taking a look at the radiator. He glanced around him at the desert. "There's no water here."

He thought for a while, then came to a decision.

"I'll tell you what. . . . You stay here and look after the truck, and I'll go and get help. I'll take the money with me because you never know who might turn up. There's all sorts of people roaming around the steppe. So remember. You wait for me."

He took the bundles of notes from the brief case, stuffed them inside his shirt, and walked away with long, purposeful strides.

I was alone, without food or water in the middle of the huge steppe.

Twice the sun rose and went down.

I wandered around near the truck, chewing the harsh leaves of the desert plants for their slightly acid moisture. I became delirious. Thousands of giggling demons rose before me, with thousands of meek uncomplaining women washing their feet. And all the demons cackled in triumph: "You see, he's left you, he won't come back. Now are you convinced that all men are bastards? Now do you believe me?"

But throwing myself down in despair, I pounded the ground with my fists and shouted hysterically: "I don't believe you! I don't believe you!"

And on the third night, when I was lying in the cab with no more strength left in me, two white, dazzling beams struck my face and small dark figures surrounded the truck.

The door flew open, two familiar, tattooed hands were around me, and I recognized the driver's face with its solid row of steel teeth. He was weeping with joy and shouting: "He's alive! He's alive!"

A tattooed hand put a bottle to my lips and poured milk into my mouth.

Since then, many demons have come my way and, no doubt, many others will, but not one of them will ever shake my faith in my fellow men.

LATER ON I JOINED ANOTHER GEOLOGICAL EXPEDITION,

this time in the Altai region. Having started as a laborer, I had become a member of the technological intelligentsia—I was a collector.

Although I came across many bad people, I grew more and more convinced that the good were in the majority. I still believe this today. Unfortunately I also noticed that the wicked usually hang together even when they hate each other. This is their strength. Good people, however, are more scattered and this is their weakness.

I also arrived at a new and different yardstick by which to measure a man's culture. I became convinced that culture is not the sum of what a man knows but his ability to sort people out, to understand them and to help them.

From this point of view many of the most educated people I met were much less cultured than ignorant soldiers, peasants, workers, and even criminals.

For me the aristocrats of the spirit are not those who can quote from books for hours on end, starting with Plato and ending with Kafka and Joyce.

For me the aristocrats of the spirit are those whose hearts are open to others. To my mind, even the most educated people, if their education doesn't stop them from being scoundrels or even helps them to be scoundrels more successfully, are the rabble. . . .

SUNBURNT AND MORE MATURE, I RETURNED TO MY MOTHER.

She met me at the railroad station and we went home by streetcar, talking of many things.

Suddenly I saw that all the passengers were staring at me in surprise and my mother was crying.

It appeared that, in talking to her, I had used without thinking a number of unprintable expressions which the companions I had just left would have taken for granted.

But they made my mother cry.

And from that day on I never swore again. Well—hardly ever.

When we got home I unstitched my trousers where I had sewn up the money I had so honorably earned and tossed it on the table.

"Whatever will you do with it?" asked my mother, throwing up her hands.

"First I'll buy myself a typewriter," I said. "The rest is for you."

No longer forced to attend school, I wrote furiously and began again to bombard the magazines with my poems. But the typewriter was no help—the poems remained unpublished.

But besides poetry, I had still another passion—soccer.

At night I wrote poetry and in the daytime I played soccer in backyards and on empty lots. I came home with torn trousers, battered shoes, and bleeding knees. The thud of the bouncing ball was, to me, the most intoxicating of all sounds.

To outflank the opponents' defense by feinting and dribbling and then to land a dead shot into the net past the helplessly spread-eagled goalkeeper, this seemed to me—and still does—very like poetry.

Soccer taught me many things.

When, later, I was goalkeeper myself, I learned to detect the slightest movement of the opposing forwards and often to anticipate their feints.

This was to be of help to me in my literary struggle.

I was told that I could make a brilliant career as a soccer player.

Many of the boys I played with at school became professionals. On the rare occasions when I meet them now, I have a feeling that they envy me, but at times I catch myself envying them.

Soccer is in many ways easier than poetry. If you score a goal you have concrete evidence—the ball is in the net. The fact is indisputable. (The referees may, in fact, disallow the goal, though this rarely happens.) But if you score a goal in poetry, you are very likely to hear thousands of referees' whistles shrilling out to disallow it—and nothing can ever be proved. And very often a shot that passed far outside the goalposts is declared a goal.

In general, in spite of all the intrigues and the dirt that go with it, sport is a cleaner business than literature. There are times when I am very sorry I did not become a soccer player.

I very nearly did.

After I had distinguished myself in a boys' match—I blocked three penalty kicks in succession—the coach of a famous team asked me to come and see him. All the other boys were green with envy.

But then something happened which determined my fate.

I had long been meaning to take my poems to the editor of Soviet Sport—it was about the only paper I had never sent them to.

I went there after the match, in a faded blue soccer shirt, old flannel trousers, and torn sneakers. I had in my hand a poem, à la Mayakovsky, in which I subjected the mores of Soviet and American athletes to a scathing analysis.

The editorial office of Soviet Sport was a big room in Dzerzhinsky Street where, through clouds of cigarette smoke and the clicking of typewriters, scratching of pens, and rustling of galleys I barely made out the presence of several figures.

I asked timidly where the poetry section was. Somewhere in the fog a voice barked that there was no such section.

Suddenly a hand, thrust out of the fog, fell on my shoulder and a voice asked: "Poetry? Let's have a look. . . ."

I trusted the hand and the voice at once, and I was right.

Before me sat a man of about thirty with raven black hair and dark Oriental eyes. He was Nikolay Alexandrovich Tarasov, in charge of four departments of *Soviet Sport*: foreign news, politics, soccer, and literature.

He made me sit down next to him and ran his eyes over my poem.

"Got any more?" he asked without comment.

I pulled out the dog-eared notebook I carried inside my belt and said, embarrassed: "It isn't about sport."

He smiled. "All the better."

He read aloud against the clatter of the typewriters. At one point he called a woman over and read her a line which compared a bunch of grapes to a cluster of balloons.

As he went on reading, several people—reporters, photographers, typists—came and stood around the desk and listened.

Finally he turned to them. "Well? Is he going to write or not?"

"He is," they said.

A hand slapped my shoulder. "He certainly is."

"I think so too," Tarasov said smiling.

To this day it beats me how they could have seen a poet in me then. Perhaps what helped was that literature was not strictly their field and so they were not cluttered up with prejudices.

When they went back to their desks leaving me with Tarasov, he picked up my poem, "Two Kinds of Sport," and said: "It's the worst of the lot, but it's the one for us. . . ."

He wrote on it the magic, long-awaited words, "To be set," and away it sailed.

"Now don't get it into your head that your other poems are all that good. But there's a strong line here and there."

I tried to look profound, as if I knew what a strong line was.

"Which poets do you like?" Tarasov asked quietly.

I swallowed. "Mayakovsky."

"Fine, but that's not enough. . . . Do you know Pasternak?"

"Yes."

"You're lying. Even if you think you do, you don't. Listen to this."

He recited verses by Pasternak which were indeed unknown to me. "Nikolay Alexandrovich, quoting Pasternak again!" A typist jokingly shook her finger at him and pointed to a door with a large notice: "Editor-in-Chief."

"Thank goodness, we're a sports magazine," Tarasov said with a laugh.

Then he bent over my notebook and started to explain to me why he thought some lines were good and others bad. What he could not endure was limp, flaccid verse. Everything experimental, even if it verged on bad taste, he liked.

"Are you in a hurry to go anywhere?" he asked. "If not, I'd like you to meet a friend of mine." He phoned someone and after a while a man of about his own age, pale, jerky, and with an immense forehead, came into the office. Unaccountably, he had a chess board under his arm.

"My friend Volodya Barlas, a physicist," said Tarasov. "Meet Yevgeny Yevtushenko, a poet."

It was the first time I had been called a poet.

"A poet?" Barlas raised his eyebrows. "That's saying quite a lot. . . ." He smiled skeptically.

At first, for some reason, he struck me as crazy.

We left the office and walked along the street, under the young rustling leaves of the trees of that Moscow June of 1949.

"A poet," Barlas said again. "And what have you to say to the world?"

"He wants to tell the world that he's a poet, and that's something for a start," Tarasov said, coming to my rescue.

He looked nervous. Clearly this odd character with the huge forehead of a Martian and the chess board under his arm meant a lot to him. And it looked as though I meant something to him as well.

Walking on, I recited three of my poems, one after another.

"All right," Barlas said at last, giving me a piercing look. "Of course you have talent. You've got drive; there's a sort of ringing and booming in your lines. But at the moment I can't see that you have anything in mind except the wish to convince the world of your talent. You haven't done it yet, of course, and you won't have an easy job. But suppose the world believes in you— then it will expect you to say something really important. What will you say to it then?"

"Volodya, he's not quite sixteen," Tarasov said, once again defending me.

"That's the time to think about it. Afterward it will be too late," Barlas said harshly.

"It will come of itself. The important thing for him now is to write and to think of nothing else. You make much too much of the rational element in poetry," objected Tarasov.

"Nothing comes of itself. . . . Emotion is fine, but emotion by itself isn't enough. . . ."

I will always thank my lucky stars for my meeting with these two men. In many ways it determined the course of my career. Once, they had both wanted to become writers but so far neither had succeeded. And now they saw in me their own youth and wanted me to fulfill its frustrated promise. We spent all night wandering about the Moscow streets. As we were saying good-by at dawn, Tarasov looked at his watch and said with warmth: "Well, in another hour the paper will be out and your poem will be in it."

"Remember—you no longer belong just to yourself," Barlas repeated his warning. But I took no notice of the alarming words.

I parted from my new friends and hung around the street, like the drunks outside the closed doors of the beer halls. My heart was pounding wildly as I waited for the newsstands to open.

At seven o'clock I snatched from the newsboy's hand a copy of *Soviet Sport* still smelling of printer's ink, unfolded it, and found my poem with my name printed underneath it.

I bought up about fifty copies—all the newsboy had—and strode down the street, waving them at the sky.

The ground whirled under my feet.

I was a genius.

I came home to my mother and triumphantly spread the paper before her. Mother's reaction could hardly be described as joyful.

"Well, there's no hope for you now," she commented with a discouraged sigh.

She may have been right at that.

Later that day Tarasov saw to it that I was paid—I got 350 rubles. As I had no identity card yet, I had to produce my birth certificate for identification. The girl in the accounting department stared at my T shirt, my torn sneakers, and my sunburnt, ridiculously peeling nose and tried hard not to laugh.

"He's a real ugly duckling," I heard her say behind my back. But I put my money in my trouser pocket, said good-by politely, and walked out like a swan who would one day be recognized.

I was told by my mother and I had read in books that all poets are drunkards. So, since I was now a poet, I decided to spend the money I had earned on drink. I consulted a friend of mine, the fourteen-year-old son of our Tatar janitor, on how best to do this. He said authoritatively that we must, of course, go to a restaurant and, naturally, be accompanied by women.

We invited two seventeen-year-old girls to play the part of the gay companions—one worked at a hairdresser's and the other was a milling-machine operator in a factory—and on their suggestion the four of us set out for the Aurora Restaurant.

This rowdy, vulgar restaurant, with its huge caryatids and with little Cupids fluttering on its ceilings, seemed to me a new and magical world.

Going through the menu I saw a wine described as "dry" and immediately ordered it. When the bottle came I was terribly disappointed. I had felt sure it was a wine served in tablets.

In the early hours of the morning I was delivered home to my mother by the girls. After my visit to the world of magic, I felt as if my guts were being turned inside out.

My mother cried. I had completely forgotten that at ten o'clock I was to meet the soccer coach at the stadium and be tried out for his team.

I got up with a splitting headache and dragged myself to the stadium.

I stood there between the goalposts without a notion of what was going on, seeing two and even three balls at a time. I didn't stop a single one of them.

The coach asked me with sympathy: "Aren't you feeling well?" He came close to me and fell back appalled.

He threw up his hands and, turning to the players who stood motionless with amazement, he delivered what was almost a Shakespearian soliloquy:

"At ten o'clock in the morning! A child of fifteen—dead drunk! I am ashamed to be living in this decadent age!"

Such was the inglorious end of my career as a soccer player.

AS I HAVE ALREADY SAID, THESE TWO MEN,

Tarasov and Barlas, whom I met in 1949, played a tremendously important formative role in my life as a man and as a poet.

With my unsettled character, I still cannot understand how they could have taken so much trouble with me and had so much patience.

Barlas was, for me, a living encyclopaedia. He opened my eyes to the basic principles of modern philosophy. He told me about Hemingway. It is only now that Hemingway is published in Russia in editions of millions of copies. At that time his books were collectors' rarities. A *Farewell to Arms*, *The Sun Also Rises*, *To Have and Have Not*, *The Snows of Kilimanjaro*, shook me by their extreme terseness and what seemed to me their concentrated virility.

Later on, *For Whom the Bell Tolls* became my favorite Hemingway novel. Some people in the West regard it as second-rate. I may be prejudiced, but the characters of the old woman and the girl still seem to me among the most striking in the literature of any country, while that of André Marty [5] brilliantly poses the problem of the fanatic who, whatever his objective rightness, so often becomes a criminal. This image prefigured many of the historical events of the succeeding years.

Barlas helped me to discover books, equally rare at the time, by such different writers as Hamsun, Joyce, Freud, Proust, Steinbeck, Faulkner, Remarque, Exupéry. . . .

I was spellbound by Nietzsche's almost biblical use of metaphor in *Thus Spake Zarathustra*, and I was hurt nearly to the point of tears when I learned that his books had been used as ideological weapons by the Fascists—a shocking fate indeed for this great writer!

I was overwhelmed by the spiritual loftiness of Thomas Mann's *Magic Mountain*, built, as a rock, on the sufferings of mankind.

I was intoxicated by Walt Whitman's immense reach, the turbulence of Rimbaud, the luxuriance of Verhaeren, Baudelaire's naked sense of the tragic, Verlaine's witchcraft, Rilke's subtlety, T. S. Eliot's hallucinating visions, and the healthy, peasant wisdom of Robert Frost.

The Russian classics, which had bored me at school because they were badly taught, became alive and as close to me as

[5] Head of the French Communist Party during the Spanish Civil War. —A.MacA.

friends. Their prose—Tolstoy's sentences, heavy as blocks of granite; Chekhov's rhythms, soft as autumn leaves; Dostoevsky's moaning and quivering like telegraph wires at night—revealed itself to me for the first time in all its beauty of language and depth and richness of meaning.

Pushkin, stale as breakfast oatmeal at school, cheerfully swung his strong young fist through the glass of his official portrait and stepped out of its frame, sly, daring, impudent, and smelling of snow and champagne. Lermontov, his tragic double and antithesis, leaped from the pages of anthologies, his horse in a lather, his cloak blowing in the winds of the Caucasus and in clouds of gunsmoke.

The eyes of poets—the deeply shadowed, seer's eyes of Blok; those baby blue, bewildered eyes of Yesenin; Mayakovsky's, mocking, mutinous, yet disillusioned—insistently met mine.

Pasternak was as yet unintelligible to me. He seemed to me too complicated and I lost the thread of his thought in the chaos of his imagery. Barlas read and reread his poems to me, explaining them with infinite patience. It depressed me very much that I could understand nothing. I have never had the arrogance of those who, when they fail to understand an artist, blame the artist, not themselves. With them, "I don't understand this!" has almost a self-satisfied, proud ring. That it might expose their own limitations never occurs to them. First one should try to understand. After that comes the right to praise or blame. I was rewarded by a miracle: one day Pasternak became crystal clear and ever since then he has been to me a simple poet, as simple as the sky and the earth.

Tvardovsky, on the other hand, struck me as too obvious, with the simplicity of a child's picture book. But once again

Barlas patiently explained to me that his seeming artlessness has its own subtlety and above all its everlasting seriousness. And although I still think Tvardovsky is a poet who in many ways limits himself unnecessarily, I deeply respect his work, and I very much regret that he is almost unknown to the Western public, as indeed are many other Russian poets.

So this was the time when my literary education began, and fate had sent me a superb teacher. But my education was not yet reflected in what I was writing. The lines of my development as pupil and writer ran parallel without as yet converging. *Soviet Sport* was now printing my poems almost every day. I wrote poems on soccer, volleyball, basketball, boxing, climbing, rowing, skating, as well as poems for special occasions: New Year's Day, May Day, Railwaymen's Day, Tank Corps Day, etc. This form of poetic journalism for special occasions was very common in our country and unfortunately survives even today. But at the time I was not just coldly churning out hack work.

I was writing for fun and with enthusiasm.

My ideas were completely immature. I was simply developing my poetic muscles. I swung alliterations, rhymes, and metaphors like Indian clubs. Tarasov was an excellent coach. As to what the poems were about, that seemed unimportant.

But these innocent childish games held the seeds of moral corruption. I remember Tarasov summoning me to his office by telephone. That day *Soviet Sport* was carrying my May Day verses.

"The editor-in-chief is in a panic, Zhenya," said Tarasov with an embarrassed smile. "It was discovered that there was not one mention of Stalin in your poem. . . . And it was too late to ax it."

"Well, what are we supposed to do?"

"Well, you know, Zhenya, I didn't want to bother you . . . so I added four lines to the poem myself."

"Fine, that's all right with me," I said cheerfully. With or without Stalin—it was all the same to me. I was a real brat.

Another time one of my poems appeared in *Trud*.[6]

I found some lines I had never written in it. They too were about Stalin.

I went to the *Trud* office to kick up a row.

"We did it to make your poem publishable," one of the editors said in an appeasing tone. "What's so shocking about it?"

And indeed, what *was* so shocking about it, I began to wonder. After all, I had myself worshipped Stalin since my early childhood.

I soon had a thorough understanding of the rules: for a poem to go through there had to be a few lines devoted to Stalin. This even began to seem perfectly natural to me. And so, of course, I no longer had to have such verses written for me—I wrote them myself.

I became a regular newspaper poet.

Soon, on commemorative occasions all the Moscow papers displayed my gaudy and empty poetic exercises.

I imagined that I had taken over from Mayakovsky. But this was only what I imagined. In reality I was learning not from Mayakovsky but from Semyon Kirsanov, an uncannily gifted experimental poet who was flooding the papers with his highly effective verse.

[6] *Trud* (Labor)—the organ of the Soviet trade unions.—A.MacA.

"You've learned *how* to write, Zhenya," Tarasov said to me. "Now you've got to think about *what* to write."

Barlas shook his head at me disapprovingly. "Stop fooling, Zhenya. I'm beginning to wonder if all those books I lent you weren't just a waste of time."

When I heard that, I decided to go and see my current idol, Kirsanov, a mature and graying poet, in the hope of getting his moral support. He looked at me sadly. "You thought that I would like your poems because they're like mine? That's just why I don't like them. As an old formalist I can tell you: forget about formalism. A poet has only one indispensable quality: whether he is simple or complicated, people must need him. Poetry, if it's genuine, is not a racing car rushing senselessly around and around a closed track; it is an ambulance rushing to save someone."

What Kirsanov said moved me to the bottom of my heart. But I couldn't stop and change. I was dragged along by sheer inertia.

In 1952 I published my first book of collected poems, *The Prospectors of the Future*; its azure-blue cover was in keeping with its contents. Although it was well received by the press, when I went into bookstores I saw whole rows of my *Prospectors* virginally intact.

In one store I noticed a young man looking at poetry books on the counter reserved for poetry. When he came to mine, I froze in expectation. He turned over a few pages, sighed, and put the book down on the pile.

"That's not what I was looking for," he said to the sales clerk. "There's a girl I know—a fine girl but she has become completely disillusioned. . . . I thought perhaps some poetry might help her. But I don't call any of this poetry. It's just drumbeating—that isn't going to restore anyone's faith in life."

The young man went out, dissolving in the driving snow.

I was deeply affected.

I went home, reread my book, and suddenly realized with the utmost clarity that it was of no use to anyone.

Who could care about my pretty rhymes and striking images if they were nothing but curlicues decorating a vacuum? What was all my searching for form worth if the means became an end in itself? My writing was too pretty. I was so afraid of boring the reader that I ended up boring him stiff.

I went out and wandered alone through the lights and the snow. People walked along the street, going home from work, tired, with loaves of bread or cardboard boxes of meat pies in their hands. The years of war and reconstruction, the years of great triumphs and great lies had laid their tragic shadow upon their faces. Their tired eyes and bent backs spoke of the hopelessness of ever understanding anything. And yet these people were not embittered or sullen; they were timidly kind and expected an answering kindness from the world. They were poorly dressed but there was a proud dignity in them, an unself-conscious dignity that was, perhaps for that very reason, all the greater. These people were dear to me, down to the last vein in their rough hands, to the tiniest wrinkle on their faces, weatherbeaten by the storms of our times. These people had no use for hollow pretty words. They had heard too many and had stopped believing them. The words they needed had to be simple, honest, and kind.

A drunk with a creaking artificial leg was punishing the bellows of his accordion as he walked along singing about a lonely mountain ash tree. Two women in quilted jackets and felt boots went by saying: "But suppose there's no such thing as love at all?"—"There is, Varya, there is, only you must wait. . . . Love will hear and come."

In a doorway a young man was awkwardly hugging a girl, kissing away the snowflakes caught in her hair. It occurred to me that no illusory world, however brilliantly imagined, could be more beautiful than the world of real people, building, struggling, weeping, and kissing. I felt ashamed and sad at having failed it.

I wandered on until I came to the Moskva River. As I stood on the bridge I put my hand in my pocket to take out a cigarette and felt the thick wad of rubles with which I had been paid that very day for my book.

I pulled the bills out and tossed them away. Twisting and fluttering, they flew off into the surrounding cold darkness. Of course it was a childish gesture, but I wanted to be rid of the money paid me for writing untruthfully. Now my pockets were empty.

They were to remain empty for a long time.

At first I couldn't write anything at all. I went to the Literary Institute and lived on a stipend. I was admitted to the Institute, even though I had no high school diploma, and to the Writers' Union as well—all on the strength of my book. But I knew now how little the book was worth. I wanted to write in a different way and, above all, about different things. I began to write about my doubts, about myself, about my expectation of a great love, about the difference between the true and the false, about the sufferings and sorrows of men.

71

When I took my new poems to the editors, they couldn't believe their eyes. "What's happened to you?" asked a young poet, in charge of the poetry section of one of the newspapers, who had always enthusiastically welcomed my verses whether on international themes or written for special occasions. "All this melancholy overtone worries me. You sound like an old man, Zhenya. What we need are cheerful verses, urging people on."

I had not become an old man. I had only begun to grow up. But this poetry editor had no personal experience of growing up, so when he noticed it in others he took it for premature senility. My reflections with their overtones of sadness struck him as a dangerous form of pessimism—as though it were possible genuinely to reflect on anything without sadness! People who see danger in sadness are themselves immensely dangerous to mankind. Artificial optimism doesn't make people advance; it makes them mark time. As our young poet Svetlov said: "Don't be like a certain locomotive I know which, instead of using its steam to go places, wastes it on blowing its whistle." In the long run that insistent, rosy-cheeked, false optimism—that flexing of the biceps for everyone to see—only leads to discouragement and decay. Whereas a clean, honest, unsentimental melancholy, for all its air of helplessness, urges us forward, creating with its fragile hands the greatest spiritual treasures of mankind.

A superficial optimism often has a much more depressant influence than the blackest pessimism, and, conversely, writing which may sound pessimistic because of its tragic subject may have an effect of optimism: the play by the Soviet author Vsevolod Vishnevsky is appropriately named *An Optimistic Tragedy.*

So the poet K, worried by the melancholy of my verse, was mistaken in thinking me a pessimist.

I remained as optimistic as before. But my optimism, which had been all pink, now had all the colors of the spectrum in it, including black. This is what made it valid and genuine.

But I had to fight for this interpretation of optimism. The opposition was sufficient to prevent almost all my poems from getting into print.

Soviet literary criticism was at the time dominated by the notorious theory of "no-conflict." Its proponents claimed that in our society there could be no struggle between good and bad but only between the good and the even better. When later some of us came into conflict with them, we finally succeeded in proving convincingly that there was still a possibility of clashes between good and evil, even in Soviet society.

But this took time.

Only after many important world-shaking political events had taken place could it be shown how essentially dangerous and non-Communist such optimism was.

Blankly smiling workers and collective farmers looked out from the covers of books. Almost every novel and short story had a happy ending. Painters more and more often took as their subject state banquets, weddings, solemn public meetings, and parades.

The apotheosis of this trend was a movie which in its grand finale showed thousands of collective farmers having a gargantuan feast against the background of a new power station.

Recently I had a talk with its producer, a gifted and intelligent man.

"How could you produce such a film?" I asked. "It is true

that I also once wrote verses in that vein, but I was still wet behind the ears, whereas you were adult and mature."

The producer smiled a sad smile. "You know, the strangest thing to me is that I was absolutely sincere. I thought all this was a necessary part of building communism. And then I believed Stalin."

So when we talk about "the cult of personality," we should not be too hasty in accusing all those who, one way or another, were involved in it, debasing themselves with their flattery. There were of course sycophants who used the situation for their own ends. But that many people connected with the arts sang Stalin's praises was often not vice but tragedy.

How was it possible for even gifted and intelligent people to be deceived?

To begin with, Stalin was a strong and vivid personality. When he wanted to, Stalin knew how to charm people. He charmed Gorky and Barbusse. In 1937, the cruelest year of the purges, he managed to charm that tough and experienced observer, Lion Feuchtwanger.

In the second place, in the minds of the Soviet people, Stalin's name was indissolubly linked with Lenin's. Stalin knew how popular Lenin was and saw to it that history was rewritten in such a way as to make his own relations with Lenin seem much more friendly than they had been in fact. The rewriting was so thorough that perhaps Stalin himself believed his own version in the end.

There can be no doubt of Stalin's love for Lenin. His speech on Lenin's death, beginning with the words, "In leaving us, Comrade Lenin has bequeathed . . ." reads like a poem in prose. He wanted to stand as Lenin's heir not only in other people's eyes, but in his own eyes too. He deceived himself as well as the others. Even Pasternak put the two names side by side:

> Laughter in the village,
> Voice behind the plow,
> Lenin and Stalin,
> And these verses now . . .

In reality, however, Stalin distorted Lenin's ideas, because to Lenin—and this was the whole meaning of his work—communism was to serve man, whereas under Stalin it appeared that man served communism.

Stalin's theory that people were the little cogwheels of communism was put into practice and with horrifying results.

The magnificent words written into Stalin's Constitution— "Work in our country is a matter of honor, valor, and heroism" —were sometimes made to mean that work itself, as a symbol, was more important than those who performed it. This attitude was reflected in every sphere of life and, needless to say, in art as well. The great and noble concept, "work," innocent of the implications drawn from it, was cheapened and degraded by books which reduced the whole of spiritual life to problems of the assembly line. The heroes of novels smelted steel, built houses, sowed wheat, but never thought and never loved—or if they did, it was as lifelessly as puppets.

Russian poets, who had produced some fine works during the war, turned dull again. If a good poem did appear now and then, it was likely to be about the war—this was simpler to write about.

Poets visited factories and construction sites but wrote more about machines than about the men who made them work. If machines could read, they might have found such poems interesting. Human beings did not.

The size of a printing was not determined by demand but by the poet's official standing. As a result bookstores were cluttered up with books of poetry which no one wanted. All that sold were Shipachev's *Lines about Love* and Simonov's reprinted wartime lyrics. A simple, touching poem by the young poet Vanshenkin, about a boy's first love, caused almost a sensation against this background of industrial-agricultural verse. Vinokurov's first poems, handsomely disheveled among the general sleekness, were avidly seized upon—they had human warmth. But the general situation was unchanged. Poetry remained unpopular. The older poets were silent, and when they did break their silence, it was even worse. The generation of poets that had been spawned by the war and that had raised so many hopes had petered out. Life in peacetime turned out to be more complicated than life at the front. Two of the greatest Russian poets, Zabolotsky and Smelyakov, were in concentration camps. The young poet Mandel (Korzhavin) had been deported. I don't know if Mandel's name will be remembered in the history of Russian poets but it will certainly be remembered in the history of Russian social thought.

He was the only poet who openly wrote and recited verses against Stalin ' while Stalin was alive. That he recited them seems to be what saved his life, for the authorities evidently thought him insane. In one poem he wrote of Stalin:

> *There in Moscow, in whirling darkness,*
> *Wrapped in his military coat,*
> *Not understanding Pasternak,*
> *A hard and cruel man stared at the snow.*

It only took an article in the press called, "We Are Not Going the Same Way, Leonid Martynov!" to insure that that wonderful poet would not get published for several years. Pasternak and Anna Akhmatova were doing nothing but translations. Poetry readings were rare and the public took no notice of them. Some poets wrote verses which were not meant to charm the reader but to get them a Stalin prize.

Once I happened to be at a meeting of the presidium of the Writers' Union. The discussion was about the nomination of candidates for the prize. I was truly shocked by the almost commercial spirit of the discussion.

It seemed to me that the most important thing about a book—whether people needed it or not—was being forgotten. I remember Tvardovsky getting up and irritably putting to shame the champions of one poet:

"Why waste our time on him? I could teach any village calf to write such poetry in no time!"

The poet's nomination was turned down. What did he feel after Tvardovsky's annihilating words? Shame? Sadness? Self-doubt? Nothing of the sort. His eyes flashed with malice, and he muttered as if to himself but so that everyone heard him: "Don't worry, I'll get it just the same."

A Stalin prize meant a lot: immediate and enormous reprints, photographs and enthusiastic articles in all the papers, appointment to some official post, a car, an apartment—without being on the waiting list—and possibly even a summer house. Many writers and poets didn't give a damn whether anybody read the book that got them the prize. What they cared about was the prize.

It would, however, be unfair of me to accuse everyone of having such an attitude. Many authors wrote honestly, without an eye to the award, and won it nevertheless. But there were plenty of careerists.

And while the furor over gold and silver medals was going on at the Writers' Union, the magnificent poet Boris Slutsky, who had managed to get only one poem published and that back in 1940, strode about the Moscow streets with his precise military step. Strange to say, he looked calmer and more composed than any of the nervous candidates for the prize.

Yet he didn't seem to have much reason to be calm. At the age of thirty-five, he had still not been admitted to the Writers' Union. He made a few rubles writing small items for the radio, and lived on cheap canned food and coffee, in a tiny rented room—he had no apartment. His desk drawers were stuffed with sad, bitter, grim poems, sometimes frightening like Baudelaire's. They were typed and ready, but it would have been absurd to offer them to a publisher.

Nevertheless Slutsky was serene. He was always surrounded by young poets and he gave them confidence in the future. Once, when I was whimpering with self-pity because my best poems were turned down, he quietly pulled open his desk drawer and showed me the pile of manuscripts inside.

"I fought in the war," he said. "I'm riddled with bulletholes. And I didn't fight in order to keep these poems in my desk. But everything will change. Our day will come. All we have to do is wait for that day and have something ready for it in our desks and in our hearts. Do you see?"

I saw.

I continued to write, and as I wrote I thought about the day that was to come and not about whether my verses would get into print or not.

I NOT ONLY WROTE POETRY, I ALSO TOOK PART

in various literary debates, denouncing falsity and bathos. I had no public-speaking experience whatever. Once my voice broke and I let out a squawk like a rooster. Laughter rose from the audience, I turned scarlet, and crammed the rest of my speech into a few minutes. Another time, when I attacked a poet who had won the Stalin prize twice and had published a trashy poem in *Pravda*, the chairman, a gray-haired, well-known poet, roughly cut me off saying I had run out of time. I looked at him in amazement—I knew I still had five minutes but I could not conceive that this gray-haired man, whose portraits had been familiar to me since my childhood, could be lying. Feeling crushed, I left the stage. Later I realized that he had, indeed, lied.

I knew that in the Writers' Union the majority were good and honest people. But I could not help noticing that some in positions of authority were neither gifted nor honorable. One particular playwright (I won't mention him by name; that would make me sick) was chairman of the dramatic section and bedecked with literary medals. It came to be known later that he wrote his plays with the help of "ghosts."

Unfortunately it was people such as he who sometimes made "literary policy," infecting it with evil-smelling things like anti-Semitism. It must be said that anti-Semitism is not in the least natural to the Russian people, any more than to any other people. It is always grafted on. In Russia anti-Semitism was artificially stirred up under the Tsars. It was just as artificially stirred up at various times under Stalin. But to me, both as a Russian and as a man to whom Lenin's teaching is dearer than anything in the world, anti-Semitism has always been doubly repulsive. The poet K, to whom an accident of fate had bound me in an undiscriminating schoolboy friendship, was, to put it mildly, not without this failing. He attempted to convince me that the whole history of opportunism, starting with the Bund [7] and going on to Trotsky, had a specifically Jewish basis. I argued with him until I was hoarse. He reproached me for my "political shortsightedness."

After one such argument he stayed the night. Next morning I was awakened by his shouts of joy. Dressed in nothing but his shorts, he was dancing a sort of African war dance, waving a newspaper which announced the discovery of the doctors' plot and the arrest of the plotters.

"See? What did I tell you? Jews, the whole lot of them!"

I must admit that I believed the report. It depressed me unutterably but without converting me to anti-Semitism, and I found K's happiness unpleasant to watch.

That same day, K and I went to see an old film about the Revolution. There was a scene in it of a Jewish pogrom in Odessa. When the shopkeepers and common criminals moved across the screen shouting, "Kill the Jews—save Russia!" and

[7] Jewish socialist organization.—A.MacA.

carrying in their hands cobblestones sticky with the blood and hair of Jewish children, I leaned toward my poet friend and asked: "Do you really want to be like them?"

He drew sharply away from me and said in a hard cold voice: "We are dialectical materialists. Not everything from the past should be discarded, Zhenya."

His eyes flashed hatred.

His Komsomol badge shone on the lapel of his coat.

I looked at him in horror; I couldn't understand what sort of a man this was, sitting next to me.

He was only twenty-four. He had not been brought up under a Tsarist tyranny, but under the Soviet regime based on the principles of internationalism. On the wall above his desk hung portraits of Lenin and Mayakovsky. How could he unite in himself two such mutually exclusive notions as communism and anti-Semitism?

Now that ten years have gone by, I realize that Stalin's greatest crime was not the arrests and the shootings he ordered. His greatest crime was the corruption of the human spirit. Of course Stalin never himself preached anti-Semitism as a theory, but the theory was inherent in his practice. Neither did Stalin in theory preach careerism, servility, spying, cruelty, bigotry, or hypocrisy. But these too were implicit in Stalin's practice. This is why some people, such as the poet K, began to think and act in an anti-Communist way though they regarded themselves as the most orthodox of Communists.

I came to realize that those who speak in the name of communism but in reality pervert its meaning are among its most dangerous enemies, perhaps even more dangerous than its enemies in the West.

From that day on, the poet K became for me the enemy of communism, and therefore my own enemy as well. (In this the attitude of some dogmatists I have met differs from mine —they regard their own enemies as the enemies of communism.)

I realized that a struggle lay ahead, a struggle to the death with those who preach communism in theory and discredit it in practice. I foresaw that the struggle would be long and difficult. Whenever people who regard communism as their own private monopoly are accused of perverting Lenin's ideas, they turn and accuse their attackers of the same thing.

Thus the poet K often reproached me with my loss of revolutionary vigilance. He never suspected that revolutionary vigilance had become my spiritual motto—as applied, among other things, to such people as himself.

It was with the vigilance of a revolutionary that I watched the erection in Moscow of blocks of tall apartment houses destined for the bureaucratic élite, while thousands of Muscovites lived in tiny, wretched, overcrowded rooms.

It was with the vigilance of a revolutionary that I read the barely disguised anti-Semitic articles in the press.

With revolutionary vigilance I noted such facts as, on the one hand, the privileged position of certain officials who, besides their salaries, received supplementary sums of sometimes double their salaries (the so-called "blue envelopes") and, on the other, the underprivileged position of those in the low-paid professions.

With revolutionary vigilance I observed the officials' distrust of simple people and their blind faith in all words which came "from above." Such current expressions as "up there they know better" or "we await instructions from above" made me all the more indignant the more common they became. "If there is an 'above' and 'below' in this almost social sense, this is surely in contradiction to every Communist principle," my revolutionary vigilance insisted.

And this vigilance, although it didn't as yet insist, already whispered in my ear:

"You do love Stalin, you trust him, don't you? But look around you: his portrait hangs in every room, they show him on the stage and on the screen, innumerable poems are written in his honor, every paper every day mentions him at least a hundred times, he is everywhere in bronze, in plaster, or in stone. Would Lenin have allowed such a thing? Is it possible that he is not the ideal person you believed? Is it possible that what is happening is his fault?"

I brushed the whispering aside, but it came back. I drove it away. It was too frightening. . . . But inside me the conviction that it was my duty to fight to remove the dirt that was about to drown the ideals of my two vanished grandfathers was growing.

I did not yet see what role poetry could play in that struggle for purification.

I confined my war to literary discussions at which I delivered angry, biting speeches, while my poetry was quiet, gentle, intimate. Of course to write such poetry was to take part in the same struggle in another form, but this form of it was passive. I felt that while it was my civic duty to become involved in the social struggle, my poetry should remain above it. Thus my thoughts about the social struggle and my poetry existed separately.

83

Readers were beginning to respond a little to my poems.

"This is all very well," said Slutsky one day after I had read him a whole pile of poems about love, "but to be a poet in our time, it's not enough only to be a poet. . . ."

I don't think I quite understood him then.

ON MARCH 5, 1953, AN EVENT TOOK PLACE WHICH shattered Russia—Stalin died. I found it almost impossible to imagine him dead, so much had he been an indispensable part of life.

A sort of general paralysis came over the country. Trained to believe that they were all in Stalin's care, people were lost and bewildered without him. All Russia wept. And so did I. We wept sincerely, tears of grief—and perhaps also tears of fear for the future.

At a meeting of the Writers' Union poets read their poems in honor of Stalin, their voices broken by sobs. Tvardovsky, a big and powerful man, recited in a trembling voice.

I WILL NEVER FORGET GOING TO SEE STALIN'S COFFIN. I was in the crowd in Trubnaya Square. The breath of the tens of thousands of people jammed against one another rose up in a white cloud so thick that on it could be seen the swaying shadows of the bare March trees. It was a terrifying and a fantastic sight. New streams poured into this human flood from behind, increasing the pressure. The crowd turned into a monstrous whirlpool. I realized that I was being carried straight toward a traffic light. The post was coming relentlessly closer. Suddenly I saw that a young girl was being pushed against the post. Her face was distorted and she was screaming. But her screams were inaudible among all the other cries and groans. A movement of the crowd drove me against the girl; I did not hear but felt with my body the cracking of her brittle bones as they were broken on the traffic light. I closed my eyes in horror, the sight of her insanely bulging, childish blue eyes more than I could bear, and I was swept past. When I looked again the girl was no longer to be seen. The crowd must have sucked her under. Pressed against the traffic light was someone else, his body twisted and his arms outflung as on a cross. At that moment I felt I was treading on something soft. It was a human body. I picked my feet up under me and was carried along by the crowd. For a long time I was afraid to put my feet down again. The crowd closed tighter and tighter. I was saved by my height. Short people were smothered alive, falling and perishing. We were caught between the walls of houses on one side and a row of army trucks on the other.

"Get those trucks out of the way!" people howled. "Get them out of here!"

"I can't do it! I have no instructions," a very young, tow-headed police officer shouted back from one of the trucks, almost crying with helplessness. And people were being hurtled against the trucks by the crowd, and their heads smashed. The sides of the trucks were splashed with blood. All at once I felt a savage hatred for everything that had given birth to that "I have no instructions," shouted at a moment when people were dying because of someone's stupidity. For the first time in my life I thought with hatred of the man we were burying. He could not be innocent of the disaster. It was the "No instructions" that had caused the chaos and bloodshed at his funeral. Now I was certain, once and for all, that you must never wait for instructions if human lives are at stake—you must act. I don't know how I did it, but working energetically with my elbows and fists, I found myself thrusting people aside and shouting: "Form chains! Form chains!"

They didn't understand me. Then I started to join neighboring hands together by force, all the while spitting out the foulest swearwords of my geological days. Some tough young men were now helping me. And now people understood. They joined hands and formed chains. The strong men and I continued to work at it. The whirlpool was slowing down. The crowd was ceasing to be a savage beast. "Women and children into the trucks!" yelled one of the young men. And women and children, passed from hand to hand, sailed over our heads into the trucks. One of the women who were being handed on was struggling hysterically and whimpering. The young police officer who received her at his end stroked her hair, clumsily trying to calm her down. She shivered a few times and suddenly froze into stillness. The officer took the cap off his straw-colored head, covered her face with it, and burst out crying.

There was another violent whirlpool further ahead. We worked our way over, the tough boys and I, and again with the help of the roughest curses and fists, made people form chains in order to save them.

The police too finally began to help us.

Everything quieted down.

"You ought to join the police, Comrade. We could use fellows like you," a police sergeant said to me, wiping his face with his handkerchief after a bout of hard work.

"Right. I'll think it over," I said grimly.

Somehow, I no longer felt like going to see Stalin's remains. Instead, I left with one of the boys who had been organizing chains. We bought a bottle of vodka and walked to our place.

"Did you see Stalin?" my mother asked me.

"Yes," I said coldly, as I clinked glasses with the boy.

I hadn't really lied to my mother. I had seen Stalin. Because everything that had just happened—that was Stalin.

THAT DAY WAS A TURNING POINT IN MY LIFE

and therefore a turning point in my poetry as well. I realized that there was no one to do our thinking for us now, if indeed there ever had been. I realized that we needed now to do some hard thinking on our own. . . . A feeling of responsibility, not only for myself but for our whole country, came upon me and I felt its crushing weight on my shoulders. Now, I don't mean that I instantly became aware of the full measure of Stalin's guilt. I still continued to idealize him to some extent. Many of Stalin's crimes were as yet unknown. But one thing was clear to me—that a great number of problems had come to a head in Russia and to refuse to try to solve them would itself be criminal.

So I thought about poetry—both my own and Russian poetry in general.

Perhaps more than the poets of any other nation, Russia's poets have been remarkable for their high civic spirit. Pushkin, for one, could evoke the most subtle world of intimate feeling while at the same time he could turn out the most biting political verse.

> *While freedom still in us does glow,*
> *And while our hearts for honor live,*
> *We'll on our land our hearts bestow,*
> *And all our noble striving give!*

This was a whole revolutionary program for the young and progressive Russia of that time. And although these lines have been greatly overquoted by now, they remain the program of Russia's youth today.

It is no accident that Russia's tyrants regarded Russian poets as their most dangerous enemies. They feared Pushkin, they feared Lermontov, and, later, they feared Nekrasov. It was Nickolai Nekrasov who wrote the couplet that is equally valid today:

> *You may or may not be a poet,*
> *But a citizen—that you must be!*

Even Alexander Blok, with his magic powers as a lyric poet, forgot his preoccupation with the everlasting enigma—woman—

and spoke in a prophetic voice about his country. Finally in Mayakovsky all this was embodied on a gigantic and revolutionary scale:

I want the pen to be equated with the bayonet . . .

To a Russian the word "poet" has overtones of the word "fighter." Russia's poets were always fighters for the future of their country and for justice. Her poets helped Russia to think. Her poets helped Russia to struggle against her tyrants.

After Stalin's death, when Russia was going through a very difficult moment of her inner life, I became convinced that I had no right to cultivate my private Japanese garden of poetry. And the great Russian poets came to my help, showing me by their example that civic poetry can be the most moving and intimate of all if the poet gives his whole heart and his whole talent to it unstintingly.

To write only of nature or women or *Weltschmerz* at a time of hardship for your countrymen is almost amoral.

And it was a time of hardship for the Russians.

THE DOCTORS WHO HAD BEEN ARRESTED IN CONNECTION

with the concocted "Doctors' Plot" were freed. The news stunned the general public who, by and large, had believed in their guilt. The trusting Russian people were beginning to understand that it could be dangerous to trust too much.

I saw the vulture face of Beria, half hidden by his scarf, glued to the window of his limousine as he drove slowly along the curb, hunting a woman for the night. . . . The same man would deliver before the people the most moving speeches about communism.

The bullet lodged in Beria's head was an act of justice—but how belated! Unfortunately justice is like a train that's nearly always late.

Rehabilitated prisoners, back from remote concentration camps, were beginning to be seen in Moscow. With them arrived news of the gigantic scale of the injustices committed.

The people were thoughtful, tense. The tension was felt everywhere. It could not be relieved by the speeches of Malenkov, a man with a womanish face and a studied diction who promised them more food, more clothes.

"Suppose we do gorge ourselves on pastry and put on new suits, where shall we go in them?" the factory worker who lived next door to us asked sarcastically.

What the Russian people wanted was for someone to say openly and seriously how they were going to live. They had never reduced the notion of "living" to food, housing and clothing. For them "living" had always included "believing."

I felt completely at a loss.

I felt there was something very important that needed to be put into words for them, but I didn't yet know what it was.

At first I thought this tension existed only in Moscow, in the welter of political events, which chased and lashed one another on. Perhaps deep in the Russian provinces there was peace and spiritual balance. I took the train to Zima Junction. I wanted to escape from my own brooding which led to conclusions that frightened me. But even on the way there, in the train, I discovered that the group of engineers and agronomists sitting near me was tormented by the same misgivings.

And when I arrived in Zima, I found them again in the first questions put to me by my two uncles—one was the head of the local car pool, the other a locksmith. I had come home to find the answers to the questions that worried me, but they were asking me for answers to the same questions. In Moscow and in Zima people were thinking about the same things. The whole of Russia was one immense sea of doubt stretching all the thousands of miles between the Baltic and the Pacific.

The image of the "simple Soviet man" has been created by our press. Songs have been composed about him, books written, and films made. The "simple Soviet man" was proudly mentioned in political speeches. But I saw how far from being simple he really was. And this made him all the dearer to my heart.

All these many different questions were like writing on the wall—"Mene, mene, tekel, upharsin"—its fiery letters blazed on the marble walls of Moscow's tall buildings and on the wooden walls of Siberian huts.

I began to write a poem, "Zima Junction." Its pages reflected the disturbing fiery glow of the same questions. I wanted to get at the very essence of what was happening.

Something, I knew, was breaking down.

But at the same time I was touching the enormous inherent spiritual strength of the Russian people who were slowly beginning to recover their freedom.

No, Russia was not a Babylon falling in ruins!

The Babylon that was falling to pieces on Russian soil was the gilded papier-mâché city of lies, built upon gullibility and the habit of blind obedience.

It was as if a blind people were recovering its sight.

People, used to keeping silent even in their own homes, had begun to talk; they talked among themselves even about the most controversial problems.

But what threatened them now was the danger of swinging over from blind faith to complete absence of faith. This was a great danger, particularly for the young.

Once in Moscow in 1954 I was spending the evening with some student friends. We were drinking cider, eating eggplant spread, reading poetry and arguing. Suddenly a girl of eighteen said in the hollow voice of a sixty-year-old ventriloquist: "The Revolution is dead."

At this another eighteen-year-old girl with a round childish face and a thick red plait got up. Her slanting Tartar eyes flashing, she said: "You ought to be ashamed of yourself. The Revolution isn't dead; the Revolution is sick, and we must help it!"

This was Bella Akhmadulina, whom I married a few weeks later.

Bella is a gifted poet. Of all the Rùssian women poets, I would put her talent second perhaps only to that of Akhmatova or of Tsvetayeva.

It was to Bella, to her Tartar eyes with their look of perpetual, quivering astonishment, that I recited the opening stanzas of my "Zima Junction." It was to those eyes that I tried to explain that the only way to save the young from skepticism was by restoring the purity of our revolutionary ideals. Her eyes understood me. The young must not be left unarmed in this fight. They must be given weapons in their struggle for the future.

By then, personal, intimate poetry, which had been almost taboo under Stalin, had broken through; it was flooding newspapers and magazines. But it was no longer so popular. In the face of the gigantic events taking place in our country, it seemed childish.

We had flutes aplenty. What we needed now was a trumpet.

Martynov's book, published at last, was strictly a flute, but the young people heard in it a trumpet call, since that was what they so passionately wished to hear. Perhaps the complexity of his metaphors and hyperbole made them read much more into his poems than was there. So to his own surprise, the voice of Martynov the lyricist resounded like the voice of a civic poet in the turbulence of those times. "A surprisingly strong echo," Martynov himself said. "It must be the times we live in."

Indeed, by its political echo even a softly uttered truth became a roar.

Slutsky began to be published. Many of his best poems were still being circulated privately, and perhaps partly because of this, political overtones were read into his published work.

But something more open, more harsh, I felt, was needed. There was of course the danger of falling into rhetoric. But one day when the poet Sukonin and I were going through an anthology of early revolutionary verse, we were amazed at how forceful it was in spite of being written in a frankly rhetorical manner. I could see that there are different kinds of rhetoric. The words "Communism," "Revolution," "Soviet regime,"

93

"May Day" sounded in these poems with all the moving purity of their first beginning. I thought that many dirty hands had desecrated our banner and that the banner itself was innocent.

It was our duty to rub off these dirty marks from our banner and to restore the original meaning to our revolutionary concepts. For this, poems needed to be written with the simplicity and force of revolutionary proclamations.

I wrote the first of a series of civic poems on cleansing the ideals of the Revolution.

In this poem I described a real incident during the May Day parade, when the loud-speakers give directions to the columns marching through Red Square:

> *Quiet please!*
> *Keep in order!*
> *No flowers?*
> *Where are the flowers?*

The poem traveled vainly from editor to editor and at one point fell into the hands of the poet K, whom I hadn't seen for a long time. I ran into him in the corridor of the magazine office where he was working and he asked me into his room, sounding as if an atomic war was going to break out the next minute.

"Do you realize what you've written?" he asked ominously.

"A poem," I replied.

"Don't you see that if that poem falls into the hands of our enemies in the West, they can use it against us?"

It bored me to talk to this man. Lenin once said that our enemies would always eat the crumbs of self-criticism that fall from our table. In fact, they clearly do. But what are we to do to stop them? Keep silent about our mistakes, about the failings of our society? A strong man is not afraid of showing his weaknesses. I believed then and I believe now in the spiritual strength of our people and I therefore regard it as my duty to speak openly about whatever I think is wrong. This precisely is my way of expressing my love for the people and my unlimited trust in them.

POETRY DAY,
WHICH WAS LATER TO BECOME
a national institution, was held for the first time in 1955. On that day poets stood behind the counter in all the Moscow bookstores, read their poems, and signed copies of their books. Several of us read our poems in a store in Mokhovaya Street, not far from the university.

I had no idea of what was coming.

About four hundred people squeezed into the bookstore which was bursting at the seams. Outside, a crowd of more than a thousand who could not get in were chanting in chorus: "Come outside! Come outside!"

We were literally carried out of the store and swept up the steps of the university. We began to read our poems. We all felt that something important was being expected of us. Love lyrics were applauded but the same expectation still shone in the eyes of our listeners. It came my turn. In front of me were fifteen hundred pairs of eyes and Bella's eyes were among them. I read the poem which the poet K had said was written for our enemies. But the young people who heard it took it not as an attack upon our country, but as a weapon in the struggle against those who were holding her back. . . . And fifteen hundred pairs of hands, raised in applause, voted for that struggle.

With the backing of the young, I wrote poem after poem calling for recruits to our side. Snobs reproached me with giving up "pure art." Dogmatists said menacingly that I was a "Nihilist." But I didn't give a damn about any of them. What mattered to me were all those young eyes turned to me, waiting expectantly.

I saw that they needed my poetry, and that, by speaking of what was wrong with our society, I was strengthening, not destroying, their faith in our way of life.

The Soviet press, radio, and television were quite obviously failing to keep up with the rapid changes in the life of the country. The nation was demanding the truth about itself from its writers.

Literary criticism was lagging hopelessly behind events.

Fiction was on the move, but slowly.

But poetry had mobility.

To begin with, a poem takes much less time to write than a novel, and it can be read in public even before appearing in print. So I chose the public platform as the battlefield on which to defend my views.

I read poetry in factories, colleges, research institutes, in office buildings and in schools. The audiences numbered from twenty to a thousand. At that time poetry readings were hardly ever allowed in the big concert halls and I could not imagine that in

1963 they would draw fourteen thousand people to the Sports Palace.

The tradition of public poetry readings, started by Mayakovsky and later given up, was being gradually re-established. But it was not on anything like the scale it has reached now—unknown even in Mayakovsky's lifetime.

It took time and determination.

The Twentieth Congress, at which the Party, showing that it had confidence in the people and was not afraid of hostile misinterpretations abroad, gave out the story of Stalin's crimes, strengthened my conviction that the people want only the truth and to keep it from them is to insult them by saying that they cannot be trusted.

Although I had some idea of Stalin's guilt, I could not imagine, until Khrushchev made his speech, how tremendous it was. Most people had the same experience. After the text was read to them at Party meetings they went away, their eyes on the ground. Probably many among the older people tortured themselves with the question: had they lived their lives in vain? The gifted writer Fadeyev shot himself with the gun he had carried as a partisan in the Civil War. His death was another of Stalin's crimes.

A part of the younger generation naturally looked with suspicion not only on Stalin but on the past as a whole, and this doubled the distress of their parents. But there were parents and parents, children and children.

The older generation split in two: the genuine, dedicated Communists who continued to work without losing heart but were ready to remember past mistakes in order to correct them; and the dogmatists who naturally regarded themselves as the most dedicated Communists of them all. But the dogmatists only paid lip service to the resolutions adopted by the Twentieth Congress to "restore the Leninist norms of life." The very word "restore" was an implicit indictment—you can only restore what is in ruins—but they lacked the civic courage to accept this fact. If they did, their leather chairs might be kicked out from under them.

They did their tricky best to balance the accounts of the Stalin era; actually, they tried to sabotage economic reconstruction. They opposed the abolition of privileges for high officials, such as the blue envelopes and the "private" chauffeur-driven cars. They grumbled and accused the younger generation, almost wholesale, of being "Nihilist" and of lacking respect for revolutionary traditions. That young men wore narrow trousers and liked jazz, or even that they read Hemingway and admired Picasso, was evidence of their "Nihilism"—and, considered sociologically, proved the contaminating effect of bourgeois influence.

What were the young people really like?

It is true that some of them became cynics. It is true that, feeling they were living in a moral vacuum, these young boys and girls chewed gum, wore sweaters and sneakers, collected records, and danced to rock 'n' roll in the belief that these were the keys to Western culture. This group usually knew nothing of Picasso and Hemingway, but they received a great deal of attention from the Western press.

In reality, they were a fairly small group.

The best of the young Soviet generation emerged from their difficult moment of doubt and reappraisal without becoming cynical. Their experience tested and strengthened their courage not only to oppose the repetition of their fathers' mistakes but also to fight for the carrying forward of their fathers' great achievement. The antagonism between the old and the new generations in the Soviet Union has been very much exaggerated in the Western press. I feel and have always felt toward many Communists old enough to be my father as if they were my contemporaries, while to me certain of my contemporaries smell of mothballs.

There seems to me to be only one way of being young: it is to be young spiritually. This is the youthfulness that unites the best of my own and of the older generation in their struggle and their work. The best of the younger generation may wear narrow trousers, like jazz music, even dance to rock 'n' roll, but this does not in any way prevent them from believing in the Revolution. They read Hemingway, Remarque, Salinger, Kerouac, and Kingsley Amis, they see foreign films and the plays of Tennessee Williams and Arthur Miller, and they stand in an endless line when there is an exhibition of Picasso or Léger. This doesn't prevent them from criticizing what is wrong in bourgeois culture and fighting for their own socialist culture. It is only that their tastes have become more varied and their horizons have widened. This is precisely what the dogmatists refuse to see.

They have tried to make use of everything, including the tense international situation, to reverse this irreversible process.

I don't think the word "thaw," which Ilya Ehrenburg stuck so casually on this movement, is a very appropriate one. I have objected to it several times in the press and should like to object again. There is no doubt that it is spring. It is a rough spring, a difficult spring with late frosts and cold winds, a spring which takes a step to the left, then a step to the right, then a step back, but which is certain, nevertheless, to go on and take two or three steps forward. And the fact that winter should hold the earth so desperately in its grip and refuse to give it up is also quite in the order of things; but then, in the very counterattacks of winter, one can sense its growing impotence—because times have changed.

For instance, people started saying that I was in disgrace, and the French magazine *Paris Match* described me colorfully as "le poète maudit de la Place Rouge." But in fact Red Square has never cursed me—I was cursed only by the dogmatists. And they were powerless to stop my writing or publishing what I wanted to write or to publish.

In 1956 my poem "Zima Junction" came out, and a ferocious attack on it by an old Bolshevik was printed in *Komsomolskaya Pravda*; but the same *Komsomolskaya Pravda* offered me space for my poems. The reviewer accused me of being a skeptic. But thousands of letters I received from every corner of the country convinced me that my poem had been understood as I had meant it—as a call for faith. And this is what I cared about most of all.

My next book, *The Highway of Enthusiasts*, had very few reviews, but it sold out at once and its disappearance from the bookstores was the best review I could have had.

In January 1957 a cycle of my poems, attacking the personality cult, nearly got torn out of already printed copies of *Young Guard*—it seems that the editors had second thoughts. The cycle was demolished by a reviewer as "Nihilistic." But on the day the review came out I got a cable from a Soviet ship at sea: "We have read your poems. Keep it up," signed "The Crew."

So I didn't lose hope.

In 1957 the discussion of Dudintsev's book, *Not by Bread Alone,* began at the Writers' Union. At the first meeting some enthusiastic speakers described the author as almost a new Leo Tolstoy. I disapproved of this extravagant praise because I saw plenty of artistic flaws in the novel, though it had many brilliant polemical passages. After some time there was another meeting, and on this occasion Dudintsev was no longer a Tolstoy but virtually an imperialist agent. Respecting him as a fellow writer and as the good citizen I knew him to be, I spoke up in his defense.

A few days later I was expelled from the Literary Institute for "irregular attendance at lectures"—to be honest, my attendance had hardly been regular for the past four years. After that I was expelled from the Komsomol—without even being given a hearing—on the charge of "estrangement."

Life didn't look too bright to me then. But the poet Yaroslav Smelyakov, who had just returned from concentration camp and whom I met at this time, made a tremendous impression on me. He had been interned three times. A wonderfully gifted poet, he had been broken and mangled by life. But out there, in camp, under unspeakable conditions, he had written a romantic poem full of hope, full of courage and faith in the ideals of the Revolution. If it was up to me, I would give him the highest Soviet award, the Order of Lenin, for that poem, which I consider a feat of heroism. Seeing this man who had kept his creative spirit alive even in a concentration camp, I couldn't allow myself to fall into despair.

I went on writing, encouraged by my friends, the poets

Shipachev, Smelyakov, Lukonin, Antakolsky, Mezhirov, Vinokurov, the artists Vassiliev and Neizvestny, and my readers who conveyed their support of me by touching letters and gifts.

I was reinstated as a member of the Komsomol and afterward became secretary of its unit in the Literary Institute, a post I held for four years.

But the critics kept tearing into me. I was labeled a "bedroom lyricist," "ideological leader of the juvenile delinquents," "a decadent bourgeois," "minstrel of dirty sheets," "bard of the gutter," "a pseudo-revolutionary," etc.

But I had a strong Siberian back.

And besides, in the changed conditions in our country not even the deadliest words had the force they had had before. My verses were still printed, my books came out, and I went on reading my poems in public.

It was the sprouting time of many young talents who were later to become famous.

Yury Kazakov, formerly a cellist who, like myself and at about the same time, had been published first in *Soviet Sport* with simple tales of American athletes, was turning into an important writer with flashes of Chekhovian subtlety. Aksenov, a young doctor writing short stories between calls, was working at his "supermodern" style.

Bella Akhmadulina, a pen in her slender fingers, sat in a lecture room at the Institute, slowly tracing in her large childish handwriting poems which combined masculine power with feminine elegance. And in the lecture room next door another student, Robert Rozhdestvensky—the big hand holding his pen still dusty from playing volleyball—sat composing his rolling journalistic verse. The poet Bulat Okudzhava edited tedious manuscripts in the daytime and in the evening sat with two or three friends, some vodka, and a guitar, singing his lyrics, without suspecting that in a few years they were to be taken down and heard on thousands of tape recorders.

A lean, large-eyed, architectural student, Andrei Voznesensky, took his poems, not yet seen by anyone, to Peredelkino to read them to Pasternak.

IN THAT YEAR, 1957, I, TOO, FIRST MET PASTERNAK.

Young poets who went to visit him at his house in Peredelkino had been telling me for some time that he wanted to meet me, but I have always felt that the best encounters were those left to chance. One day, however, I was delegated by the Writers' Union to accompany the Italian professor Ripelino, who was going to call on Pasternak at his *dacha*.

We arrived without an appointment.

Suddenly, stepping out from behind a tree in the garden, a suntanned, gray-haired man in a white linen jacket almost bumped into me.

"How do you do?" he said in a slightly singsong voice, shaking my hand; his brown eyes looked astonished, yet at the same time as if they were never astonished by anything. Without letting go of my hand, he suddenly smiled and said: "I know who you are . . . you're Yevtushenko . . . yes, yes, that's just how I imagined you—thin, long-legged, trying to pretend you're not shy. . . . Well, I know all about you—I know you don't attend lectures regularly at the Literary Institute . . . and so on. . . . Is that a Georgian poet you've brought with you? I'm very fond of Georgians. . . ."

I explained that it was not a Georgian poet but an Italian professor and introduced him.

"Good, that's good, I'm very fond of Italians, too. And you've come at just the right time—dinner's just ready. Come, let's go in—I'm sure you must be very hungry."

And at once everything was quite simple and easy, and soon we were sitting at the table, eating chicken and drinking brandy.

To look at him, Pasternak might have been forty-seven or forty-eight. His whole appearance had an amazing, sparkling freshness, like a newly cut bunch of lilacs with the morning dew still on their leaves. It seemed as if there was a play of light all over him, from the flashing gestures of his hands to the surprisingly childlike smile which constantly lit up his mobile face. But he was play-acting a little.

He had once written of Meyerhold:

> *Even if you are only acting*
> *You are right. Just continue to act.*

He was saying it also of himself.
And I remember other lines by Pasternak:

> *It takes the greatest courage*
> *To go on acting to the end*
> *As do the rivers*
> *And the ravines . . .*

It must indeed have taken great spiritual courage to retain

throughout that unsmiling period the ability to smile as he did.

This ability may have been his protection.

People reacted to Pasternak not as to a man but as to a color, a smell, or a sound.

He laughed and said: "Such a funny thing happened to me today. A roofer I know came to see me. He pulled a bottle of vodka out of his pocket, and a piece of sausage, and he said: 'I did some work on your roof the other day, but I didn't know who you were. Now, some good people tell me you stand for the truth. That deserves a celebration, so let's have a drink to that.' We had a drink. Then the roofer said to me: 'Well now, you lead the way.' I couldn't understand what he meant at first. 'Where am I to lead you?' 'To fight for truth,' he said. 'You'll have to show the way.' Well, as you know, I didn't intend to lead anyone anywhere. I think a poet is just a tree—it stands still and rustles its leaves; it doesn't expect to lead anyone anywhere."

He gave us a sidelong look and asked: "Well, what do you think—is it true or isn't it that the poet is only a rustling tree and doesn't have to lead anyone anywhere?"

Selvinsky once wrote that Pasternak resembles, at the same time, both the Arab and his horse. I thought this very true.

Afterward Pasternak read us some poetry, drawling the vowels and swaying his head gently from side to side. It was "Bacchanalia," a poem he had written a short time before.

When he came to the lines:

> *For the first skirt he sees*
> *He'll leap over traces,*
> *And knock down as he flees*
> *Every barrier he faces . . .*

he looked mischievously at his wife who was fiddling nervously with the edge of the tablecloth, and he sighed cheerfully over this whiff of his wild youth, a youth that was still bubbling inside him.

He asked me to read some of my poems.

I began with "Weddings," which he didn't particularly like. Then I read "Prologue" and this he loved. He clapped his hands like a small boy when a line especially pleased him, he kept wriggling in his chair, and when I finished he rushed over and hugged me. I felt depressed, for it seemed to me that Pasternak couldn't have a good ear. "Prologue" was the more showy and the more superficial of the two poems. I realized afterward that I had been wrong. When we met again and I read him my "Loneliness," he began to cry and said: "You wrote this about me . . . about me and about us all. . . ."

Pasternak had exuberant moods, and he had liked "Prologue" because it fitted his mood at the time.

One day I'll write at length about the four occasions on which I saw Pasternak. The last time we said good-by he kissed me hard according to the Russian custom. His lips had the fragrance of lilacs.

He was a pure and innocent man. All the more criminal then were the actions of those in the West who, against his will, used his name in the cold war, and the more deplorable the actions of some of our writers who tried to strike his name from the pages of our literature.

Certainly he loved his country and he never intended to harm it in any way. There were many things he didn't understand, not because he didn't want to. He simply couldn't.

Many events in our life appeared to him as if they were

happening on the other bank of the river of time. Thanks to his uncanny vision, he could see many things distinctly through the drifts of mist which hang over the river, but the outlines were often blurred, and some things were hidden by the mist altogether.

The many years he spent in the country, hardly ever leaving Peredelkino, gave him the invaluable opportunity to be alone with himself and with nature. But his remoteness from the rush and noise of the big city subdued his sense of the urgency of the struggle in the world today. He realized this. As he put it, he was the boundary post between two epochs. And in this lies the greatness and also the tragedy of this poetic genius.

IN 1957 I MET TWO MEN WHO WERE LATER to be my close friends—the artist Yurii Vassiliev and the sculptor Ernst Neizvestny. They were older than I and had fought at the front and been wounded several times. After the war, they refused to become blind followers of the established academic style and eagerly went in search of new art forms. They thought with some justification that they had shed their blood for the right to paint and sculpt as they liked. But not everyone saw their point of view and my friends were having a hard time. . . .

Before I met them, I knew nothing about painting. The

Impressionists were the most modern painters I had seen. Like most Muscovites, I had failed to get into the Picasso exhibition when it came to Moscow—it was harder to get a ticket than to win a car in the state lottery. Of course, I had read a little in the newspapers about modern trends in art, but those who followed them were described as thoroughly dishonest people, corrupt, mercenary, and hostile to communism.

Yet here were two men who had fought in the war, who were dedicated Communists, whose honesty was unimpeachable, who were producing abstract paintings and sculptures.

Not that Vassiliev and Neizvestny are entirely abstract artists; they do a good deal of realistic work, but their realism is of today and has nothing to do with stuffy academic Soviet art. And they have experimented in abstract art.

Can a man who is a good Communist also paint abstract pictures? Several years later, in Cuba, one of the Cuban revolutionary leaders told me this story:

Before the attack on Batista's palace, a group of revolutionaries spent several days in a small house, waiting for orders. Each of them had his favorite occupation—one read, another wrote poetry, others played chess. Among the revolutionaries were two painters, a realist and an abstract artist. They painted, arguing furiously (though in view of the special conditions, in whispers) and nearly came to blows. But when the order to move out finally came, both the realist and the abstract painter went to fight for the future of their country, and both were killed.

I very much wish this story were known to those dogmatists who write off all modern artists as lackeys of bourgeois ideology. One must be more patient and more discriminating. Certainly there are frauds and profiteers who are hangers-on of modern art, but there are also many honest, hard-working people. They may sometimes wander along the wrong artistic path, but it does not necessarily follow that there is something wrong with their political ideology. It is wrong to confuse differences in artistic style with differences in ideology. I became convinced of this through my friendship with Vassiliev, Neizvestny, and other young artists. Later, when I went abroad, I met and saw the work of many Western artists, including such men as Picasso, Max Ernst, Chagall, Miro, Henry Moore, and Braque. I may disagree with them about many things but I could never slight these artists who work so hard and so richly deserve our respect.

I fell in love with painting. On the walls of my apartment I now have pictures by realists, expressionists, surrealists, and abstractionists. They don't clash with each other and they don't infect me with bourgeois ideology. These pictures are my friends and when I feel depressed I go and have a silent talk with them.

When I think of all the various isms in art, it occurs to me that realism is indeed the best of them. But realism as I understand it has hundreds and thousands of facets and it need not be representational. I see as realism whatever is genuinely begotten by life and moves the human spirit, even if there are no images of people, houses, or trees. On the other hand, if a picture has people, houses, and trees, but is lifeless and has no power to communicate with me, then it is mere abstraction and nothing else.

My idea is that we should redefine the concepts of realism and abstractionism. In the sense which I have just given, I am against abstract art.

MY FRIENDS LIKED TO DREAM.

Yurii Vassiliev's dream was that one day Beria's house would be put at his complete disposal and, out of this monument to corruption and political cynicism, he would create a palace of modern art.

Neizsvestny dreamed that he would build himself a shed on the banks of the Moskva, and inside it, in complete secrecy, he would begin to work on a gigantic statue of Liberty. He would raise the height of the shed by means of superstructures, so that it would continue to hide the statue until it was ready. Then one day he would demolish the wooden shed and Moscow, stunned, would see his creation. . . . And all the critics would bite their nails.

My friends smelled of clay and paint and the future. They worked unceasingly, infecting me with their faith and their inspiration. My wife and I had just divorced. When I was too unhappy and lonely, the example of my friends gave me strength.

What also encouraged me was the increasing interest which my readers showed in my work.

My readers felt my deep private sorrow in my poetry, and they sympathized with me. But while sympathizing with me in their letters, they also warned me not to let what I was going through stand between myself and the inner experience of the people as a whole. Thereafter when I wrote, no longer thinking only of myself, I felt that my readers were also my collaborators.

I felt the same contact with my listeners at poetry readings.

I often tried out my poems on them before they were published, reading them to people in all kinds of jobs and professions. The amount of applause only showed whether the poem pleased; the discussion that followed was what interested me.

One such discussion at the Moscow Institute of Electrical Engineering attracted nearly two thousand people—this was a record.

"You must go on writing lyrical, intimate verse; people need that too," the students said. "But remember that you no longer belong to yourself. This is not the only thing we expect from you."

Another day I read poetry to workers in a factory during their lunch hour. Both men and women listened for nearly the whole hour, forgetting their sandwiches, and when the whistle blew an elderly woman wiped her eyes on the sleeve of her overalls and said: "Read some more, dear. . . . We'll make up the time. . . ."

At the end of the reading this woman came up to me and said in a low voice: "Just write the truth, son, just the truth. . . . Look for the truth in yourself and take it to the people. Look for the truth in people and store it in yourself."

I think these were the most important words I ever heard.

Some critics tried to represent me as a hoodlum and said my poetry evenings were attended by hysterical girls with nothing better to do and by juvenile delinquents. But nothing scandalous ever happened. If the doors and windows did get smashed now and again and the police stood by to maintain order, this was only because there was not enough room.

I was in an extremely ambiguous position. Insults were hurled at me; I was showered with applause. It was enough to drive a man out of his mind, but there was always an inner voice saying to me: "When you are abused, you are not in danger. To be loved is more dangerous. You must be as clearsighted when you are loved as when you are hated. This love is only an advance payment for what they expect of you. This love is a big responsibility. Remember what you were told: you must look for the truth both in yourself and in people. . . ."

I looked for it. I discussed love and politics with tractor drivers in the virgin lands of the Altai. I argued about Stalin with fishermen on the Volga. With tiger hunters in the Far East I exchanged ideas on the best way of stopping war. I debated on the meaning of happiness with lobster fishermen on the Kamchatka peninsula, and on the meaning of poetry with winegrowers in Georgia.

Of course, I listened more than I spoke. Before you can have anything to say, you must learn to listen.

AND WHILE I WAS AWAY ON THESE JOURNEYS, in faraway Moscow newspaper articles described me, as before, as the poet who had lost contact with the people.

Once, after wandering for a long time through the taiga, I arrived in the town of Komsomolsk on the Amur River and went to see the secretary of the town's chapter of the Komsomol. When I gave my name, his eyes nearly popped out.

"But it's impossible—you can't be."

He handed me the Moscow paper he had just been reading. In it I was described as "the head of the intellectual juvenile delinquents" and the "idol of undiscriminating females."

The secretary looked at my face, swollen with mosquito bites. "I don't know about the women, but the mosquitoes certainly love you."

Many of the literary critics who highhandedly determine who has and who has not lost touch with the people have themselves been out of touch for a long time. One such established authority, addressing young writers, once asked them: "Why do you fellows keep flying off on official visits to places like Siberia and Kamchatka? It costs the State a lot of money. Get on a streetcar, pay your fifteen kopeks, and you can get to any factory outside Moscow."

A young writer, looking at the critic sadly, replied: "It's ten years, dear Comrade, since a streetcar ticket cost fifteen kopeks. The present price is thirty."

For some writers, their home was their world. What I wanted was that the whole world should be my home. This is why I was so drawn to visit every corner of my country. And why I was drawn beyond her frontiers.

I wrote:

> *Frontiers are in my way;*
> *It's awkward*
> *Not to know Buenos Aires*
> *Or New York.*
> *I want to knock around*
> *As much as I need in London,*

> *I want to talk to everyone*
> *Even in pidgin,*
> *I want to strap-hang like a kid*
> *Through morning Paris.*

The immediate reaction of the critics to the poem was: let his Marxist ideology be molded into its final shape first. But to begin with, what is the final shape of Marxism? No ideology which is in its final shape can be Marxist, because genuine Marxism is forever molding itself.

But by now these exhortations from those in a firm mold had lost some of their force.

I did go abroad. The first countries I visited were Bulgaria and Rumania.

In a Bulgarian village street our bus was stopped by a rope of embroidered hand towels knotted together and stretched across. There was a wedding in the village and we were invited in like brothers. We drank to the newlyweds.

I took a flask of vodka from my pocket and passed it around. A member of our tourist group said in a frightened whisper: "Whatever are you doing, Yevgeny Alexandrovich?"

I didn't know what he was talking about at the time. In the evening he came to my room and said that I had compromised the image of the Soviet citizen, and from now on Bulgarians would think that every Russian carried a bottle of vodka in his pocket. My fellow tourist's ideology had been molded in its final shape.

Such crippled minds are one of the most dreadful bequests of the Stalin era.

Under Stalin, the only people who went abroad were diplomats and members of official delegations. To many of us the outside world was wrapped in a fog of mystery. Because of this some thought it too attractive, others too dangerous. For my fellow tourist this was even true of friendly Bulgaria.

Now the fog was beginning to dissipate. Tens of thousands of foreign tourists were coming to us, and tens of thousands of our tourists were going abroad. The Moscow Youth Festival, when young people of every color and from every country flooded the streets, had tremendous importance. In it I saw a blueprint of the future. The words of Paul Eluard, "from the horizon of the individual to the horizon of mankind," echoed more and more often in me, and it seemed to me that we must struggle to unite not only the best people in our country but the best people throughout the world. That also became the aim of my poetry.

If, before, I felt a responsibility for my own country, I now felt a responsibility for the whole world. And so in every country I visited, instead of going to see the beautiful sights and historical monuments, I looked for men who were prepared to fight heart and soul against lies, the abuse of power, and the exploitation of man by man wherever they exist. And everywhere I found such men.

I spoke with students from Ghana, Togoland, and Liberia about the future of liberated Africa and drank to it out of coconut shells filled with cool coconut milk. Noticing young workmen in Paris writing "Paix en Algérie" on the wall in a side street, I went up to them, borrowed a piece of charcoal, and contributed an exclamation mark. In a big square in New York, I joined American young men and girls in singing a biting song addressed to the police commissioner who had banned their gathering. So as not to be dispersed by the police, they were carrying flags; I liked to see the American flag in hands like those.[8] In chorus with bearded Cubans I sang my favorite song, "The International." In London I marched with the ban-the-bomb demonstrators.

In Finland, when enraged hoodlums tried to wreck the Youth Festival, I wrote the poem "Snot-nosed Fascism," which, translated into several languages, was handed around to the delegations and became ammunition.

"You'll have to forgive me if I didn't have a very good opinion of you up to now," a Komsomol official in our delegation said apologetically. "I never thought you would write a poem like that. . . . Not you. Why don't you concentrate on international themes? That bit about bourgeois ideology was really good. . . ."

He was naïve. He didn't understand that I have won the moral right to talk about what is wrong abroad only because I speak just as openly about whatever I see to be wrong in my own country; otherwise I would lose my self-respect.

This man, for instance, disapproved of my poem "Babi Yar." Yet I could not have written "Snot-nosed Fascism" if I hadn't first written "Babi Yar." Both these poems are facets of the same struggle—the struggle for the future.

I had long wanted to write a poem on anti-Semitism. But only after I had been in Kiev and had seen Babi Yar with my own eyes did the poetic form come to me. I wrote the poem in only a few hours after my return to Moscow. That evening I gave a talk on Cuba at the Polytechnic Institute. After my talk I read "Babi Yar" for the first time. Ordinarily I recite my poems

[8] This was the demonstration against the police ban on folk singing in Washington Square. The American flag is required by law at public meetings. The affair had absolutely no political implications.—A.MacA.

by heart but this time I was so agitated that I had to have the text in front of me. When I finished there was dead silence. I stood fidgeting with the paper, afraid to look up. When I did I saw that the entire audience had risen to their feet; then applause exploded and went on for a good ten minutes. People leaped onto the stage and embraced me. My eyes were full of tears. Afterward a white-haired man leaning on a stick came up to me.

"I've been a Party member since 1905. Would you like me to recommend you for membership?"

Only the day before I had read a review of my poem "Consider Me a Communist." The reviewer said that if he were at a meeting when the question of admitting me to the Party were put to the vote, he would be opposed. The article was actually entitled "I Am Opposed."

Now the white-haired old man went on: "What you've said about Cuba and what you've written about Babi Yar are one and the same. Both are the Revolution. The Revolution we once made, and which was afterward so betrayed, yet which still lives and will live on. I spent fifteen years in one of Stalin's concentration camps, but I am happy that our cause, I mean the cause of the Bolsheviks, is still alive."

At this I burst into tears, though I am not usually that emotional.

I took the poem to the office of the *Literary Gazette* and read it to a friend of mine who was on the editorial staff. He rushed off next door, brought several colleagues, and made me read the poem again. Then he said: "Would you let me make a copy? I'd like to have one, and the others asked for copies too."

"What do you mean, copies? I've brought it for you to publish."

They looked at each other in silence. It hadn't even occurred to them to think of such a thing. Then one of the editors said with a bitter laugh: "He's still sitting in all of us, that damned Stalin. . . ." And he wrote on the typescript the words "For publication."

"Don't leave yet," my friend said. "The editor-in-chief hasn't seen it and there might be some questions."

For two hours I sat fidgeting. Every other minute people from various departments dropped in and said reassuring words in uncertain voices. Some typists gave me some chocolates.

An old compositor came in.

"You Yevtushenko? I want to shake you by the hand, son. I've just set your poem 'Babi Yar.' It hit the nail right on the head. All our people in the pressroom have read it, and they want you to know how much they like it."

The old man's hand dived into the pocket of his overalls and came up with a bottle of vodka and a pickled cucumber. "That's from the printers to cheer you up . . . and don't you worry. . . . I'll keep you company. Your health. . . . That's better! . . . You know, when I was young, I was in a workers' brigade. We used to stand by the Jews whenever there was a pogrom. No decent man could be an anti-Semite. . . ."

The old man went on talking and gradually the weight was lifted off my chest.

At last I was called in to see the editor-in-chief. He was a middle-aged man; from under his bushy eyebrows his eyes gave me a sly, peasant look. They were eyes that had seen plenty; they looked understanding.

"It's a good poem," he said with deliberation, weighing me.

I knew from experience that if the editor-in-chief began with those words, the poem would be turned down.

"What it says is right," he went on with equal deliberation. By now I was sure.

"We're going to publish it," said the editor-in-chief.

The slyness went from his eyes and they looked hard.

"I'm a Communist," he said. "You understand? So I can't refuse to publish your poem. Of course, anything may happen. I hope you're prepared."

"I am," I said.

"Are you going to wait for the paper to come out?"

"I am," I said. I went back to the editorial room. The paper was normally put to bed at seven. The men who had finished their work stayed on. It struck seven. But the editor-in-chief hadn't signed the order to start printing. It struck eight. The editor-in-chief sent his car to fetch his wife and daughter from his summer house. It struck nine. A good-looking young woman who was the pressroom foreman came in and put the proof sheets before me without a word. They were complete except for a blank in the space reserved for the poem. It struck ten. The old compositor brought another bottle and we drank that one up. It struck eleven. The wife of the editor-in-chief arrived. At eleven-thirty the editor called me in.

"I'll come with you," the woman foreman said nervously. "If there's trouble, I'll say it's too late to change the layout . . . or I'll think of something else. I couldn't face the men!"

We went in. The editor-in-chief and his wife were standing there looking at the proofs.

They smiled at my exhausted appearance.

The foreman saw that the sheets were initialed. She seized them and skipped out.

"I decided I'd ask my wife's advice," said the editor-in-chief. "I can always rely on her. As you see she approves. . . . You can go and watch your poem coming off the press."

I went down to the pressroom. The printers shook hands with me. The foreman gave a signal and the press started rolling. Suddenly there was a creaking and rumbling and it stopped. I had been so wound up that the interruption petrified me. The old compositor patted my shoulder. "It's all right. Just be patient for another minute."

The press started rolling again and the first copies fell at my feet.

The foreman put a batch in my arms. "You'd better hang on to them. By tomorrow they'll be collectors' items." We all hugged each other. I felt all of us had written it. My friend and I got into my battered old car. Miraculously, we discovered a bottle of Beaujolais on the seat. My friend went back to his office and brought down a pair of long editorial scissors. We got the cork out, finished the bottle in the car, and drove home. It was one in the morning.

Next morning every copy of *Literary Gazette* was sold out at every newsstand in a matter of minutes. By that afternoon I was getting batches of telegrams from strangers congratulating me. But the rejoicing was not universal. Two days later the journal *Literature and Life* published an answering poem by Alexei Markov [9] in which I was described as a "pigmy who had forgotten the people he belonged to" and in another two days a

[9] After Khrushchev's speech of March 1963, the poet Markov was named chairman of the Moscow chapter of the Writers' Union—A.MacA.

long article in the same paper accused me of trying to wreck Lenin's international policy by stirring up hatred among national groups.

A more monstrous and grotesque charge it would be hard to imagine. But the author's chauvinism was ill disguised and there was public indignation. I was showered with letters from all over the country. One morning I was visited by two young men about seven feet tall with badges inscribed "Master of sports." They said they had been sent by the Komsomol organization of the Institute to act as my bodyguards.

"To guard me?" I asked in surprise. "Who are you to guard me from?"

The young men looked embarrassed; they told me that while, of course, my poem had been very well received by the public, we had not achieved communism yet and there were still some bastards around. They faithfully kept at my heels for several days. I learned that they themselves were no great lovers of poetry, but had been chosen for their other qualities: one was a boxer, the other a wrestler. It was very funny and I was very touched.

I was not of course in any danger. Out of some twenty thousand letters written to me about "Babi Yar," only thirty or forty were abusive and they were all unsigned and in obviously disguised handwriting. In our country it is the bastards who are in danger. It was not I but Markov who had something to fear. He canceled his public appearances because the organizers of the meetings hinted that his face might be pushed in.

The Western press made a sensation of the attacks on "Babi Yar," claiming that they proved the existence of anti-Semitism in the Soviet Union, and some of these papers dishonestly distorted the meaning of my poem to suit their own ends. But as far as I was concerned, the two attacks on me in *Literature and Life* were less significant than the reaction of the wide and varied public—workers, collective farmers, intellectuals, and students—who supported me at that difficult moment. When I gave a reading in Mayakovsky Square just before leaving for Cuba, ten thousand people came to give me a marvelous send-off, and the support of the people will always mean more to me than anything else.

WHEN I WROTE MY POEM "STALIN'S HEIRS"

and began reading it publicly, someone spread the rumor that it was anti-Soviet. Those who found that the shoe fit them were afraid that others would see this too; editors were afraid to publish it. But no one dared to forbid me to read it because the audiences shouted for it, and I didn't whine when it remained unpublished for a year—I had known this would happen.

I sent the poem to Khrushchev, and it was published in *Pravda*. The dogmatists were growing more and more impotent. To the great displeasure of many of them, Solzhenitsyn's remarkable novel *One Day in the Life of Ivan Denisovich* was also published with the direct help of Khrushchev.

It goes without saying that the dogmatists used, still use, and will go on using every opportunity they can find to arrest the process of democratization in our society.

I have no rosy illusions about that.

I know equally well that the dogmatists have reared a new crop of young people to replace them. These young people are perhaps our greatest internal danger. But they are easily outnumbered by our progressive-minded young people, and there is no doubt in my mind that dogmatism is doomed.

I know that we are facing many difficulties in our national economy and in foreign relations. There are complications, too, in the development of our arts.

I don't shut my eyes to any of this.

Nevertheless, one would have to be blind not to see the immense changes in our country since Stalin's death. Indeed, what has been happening in the Soviet Union since 1953 is a spiritual revolution, one which subjects us to great tensions and which demands of us great patience. We have to tell ourselves very clearly which are the things in our past we mean to carry forward into our future and which are those we shall leave behind.

We are sometimes told that we talk too much about the past. But for us, talking about the past means thinking about the future.

We have made many mistakes. But we were the first to attempt to carry out the ideas of socialism, and perhaps our mistakes were made in order that they should not be repeated by those countries who will follow in our footsteps.

In a café in Paris a student who did less than credit to his revolutionary forebears said to me: "In general I'm for socialism. But I'd rather wait until you get stores like the Galeries

Lafayette in Moscow. After that I might consider fighting for socialism. . . ."

I felt ashamed for this senile young man.

What he wants is to have his future served to him on a silver platter, nicely cooked, brown outside and pink inside and with a sprig of parsley; then perhaps he'll pick at it with his fork. We at least are making the future ourselves, doing without the barest necessities, suffering, making mistakes, but all the same doing it ourselves.

It makes me proud not to be just an onlooker but to be taking part in my people's heroic struggle for the future.

And I want to believe that everything is still ahead of me, as it is for my people.

Translated by Andrew R. MacAndrew

Weary of being labeled pop star by some, political propagandist by others, Yevtushenko's plea today—1972—is to be regarded a poet, nothing else. Yevtushenko writes: "Before judging his age a writer must first have the courage to judge himself." (Ed.)

EPILOGUE

The last years of Stalin coincide with the earliest publications of Yevgeny Alexandrovich Yevtushenko. He had been born in 1933, long after the Revolution, the Civil War, the death of Lenin; the tense emotions of those years, or even of the Second World War, could not serve as a first-hand inspiration to him as they had done to most of the good Soviet poetry which was not of a purely lyrical nature. In Yevtushenko, born and brought up in an already securely established Soviet Union, there could be no question of an inner conflict between the attractions of the old order of society and the new, whose resolution was of such vital importance to the poets of that first era after the Revolution. The remarkable impact that Yevtushenko made sprang more than anything else from his being the representative of a new generation, seeing old truths through fresh eyes as each new generation must. By consistently refusing to compromise his regard for truth or his concept of good poetry he became this new generation's unchallenged literary spokesman, and opened a way for the host of talented young poets that has emerged in the last decade.

When asked about his early life, Yevtushenko is apt to refer the questioner to his poetry; this is indeed so autobiographical that one can learn almost everything important about the writer from it. He was born in the remote town of Zima on the trans-Siberian railway, of mixed Ukrainian, Russian, and Tartar blood, in a peasant family. "Zima Junction" vividly describes his childhood in Siberia and his return there at the age of twenty after a long absence in Moscow. His father was a geologist, and when only fifteen and seventeen years old he took part himself in geological expeditions to Kazakhstan and to the Altai. He was a considerable athlete: cycling, ping-pong, football (he was a goal-keeper) were among his favorite activities, and his first published poems were actually printed in a sporting journal in 1949. The seeds of his poetic talent had, however, been sown some time earlier, when as a child during the war he had been made to dance and sing—and found himself improvising verses. It is interesting that some of his more recent poems, though not intended specifically as songs, have been set to music and have become extremely popular in this form.

He was accepted as a student by the Moscow Literary Institute, where he achieved little success. Though he had been writing from an early age, his poetic talent took some time to mature. His first book of poems was published in 1952. Shortly afterward ensued a period of brilliant work. The years 1955-7 mark a peak of quality in his poetry; it was a prolific period—books of his verse appeared in 1955, 1956, and 1957, each better than the one before. But new-found fame and popularity had its dangers. Many Soviet literary critics, themselves relics of the deadening last years of Stalin when poetry was almost completely stifled by political dogmatism, reacted with violent hostility to the appearance of a fresh, talented, unashamedly self-confident young poet whose professed concern was to seek out truth for himself and not to have it dictated to him from above. From that time to the present he has been the subject of many hostile articles* in literary journals (for example in *Kom-*

* In 1968, Yevtushenko was attacked by British intellectuals when students named him their candidate as Oxford's Professor of Poetry. (Ed.)

somolskaya Pravda of 21 June 1957, *Literaturnaya Gazeta* of 8 April 1958, *Literatura i Zhizn* of 27 November 1961); after the publication of "Zima Junction" he had to withdraw temporarily from the Komsomol organization. But it would be quite wrong to make Yevtushenko out to be a victim of unrelenting persecution; one can also point to enthusiastic articles (e.g. in *Novy Mir*, 1957:5, and in *Literaturnaya Gazeta*, 9 January 1960). The Soviet Union is a more complex place than the West seems prepared to believe, and particularly in the literary world (where ceaseless and often fruitful controversy is carried on between highly disparate factions); to speak of any monolithic "party line" and to try and measure a writer against it is senseless.

Since 1960, Yevtushenko has traveled abroad a great deal to France, Africa, the United States, Cuba, Great Britain. Insatiably curious, open-minded, with an enormous appetite for people, he has found foreign travel enriching to him as a poet and a person, just as earlier he found excitement and inspiration in the transcaucasian Republic of Georgia. An equally potent inspiration has been his second, happier marriage to Galina Semyonovna, a fellow-Siberian (his first, to the brilliant poetess Bella Akhmadulina, dated from 1954). His recent books command printings of several hundred thousand copies, showing that (as he says himself) nowadays at last the publication of a Soviet poet is determined by the demands of the reading public rather than his place in any official hierarchy. His activity is remarkable. Apart from his large output of verse he has experimented with prose-writing and, currently, film-making; at the same time he is in enormous demand to recite his published and unpublished poetry in Russian clubs, factories, universities, and theaters—he claims to have made about 250 such readings in 1961.*

How does this poetry compare with that of his Soviet predecessors? Though fresh, it is not strikingly innovatory, and he owes a good deal to the past. It could tentatively be described as middlebrow poetry, and as such it lacks the obscurity associated with Khlebnikov and other early twentieth-century writers. Among modern poets his greatest admiration is for Blok, Mayakovsky, Yesenin, and Pasternak (whom he knew personally). He has most in common with Mayakovsky and Yesenin. Like Mayakovsky, he is by temperament a natural revolutionary, hating stagnation, bondage, hypocrisy—and with a fundamentally gentle nature, unpuritanical and libertarian, insistent that ends do not justify bad means. He owes much to Mayakovsky stylistically, above all the declamatory, powerful, colloquial aspects of his verse, whose impact often cannot be fully appreciated until it is heard aloud. Like Yesenin, he is a peasant boy who has come to the city—and for whom his remote birthplace continues to hold a deeply felt significance; vigorously sensual, often regarded by his elders as a destructive and degenerate influence (though in reality a passionate seeker after truth and moral justice). But Yevtushenko is an original poet, and cannot be fully characterized by his antecedents alone, any more than the numerous young poets now writing in the Soviet Union are to be characterized simply by reference to Yevtushenko (who nevertheless has blazed the trail for them). His work as a whole

* In New York in February 1972, Yevtushenko said he had lost his energy for marathon readings and travel. His future plans call for less poetry, a concentration on prose—especially short fiction. He writes, "To write good prose you must chain yourself down." (Ed.)

shows a fundamental feature which is typical of the best Russian poetry since early in the last century: an ability to move effortlessly from social to personal themes, from publicist to lyricist, combining them in a single poem. Other writers could learn much from him in this.

Robin Milner-Gulland and Peter Levi, S.J.

POEMS

NEW YORK ELEGY

At night, in New York's Central Park,
chilled to the bone and belonging to no one,
I talked quietly with America:
both of us were weary of speeches.

I talked with my footsteps—
unlike words, they do not lie—
and I was answered with circles
dead leaves uttered, falling onto a pond.

Snow was falling, sliding embarrassed
past bars where noisiness never ceases,
settling tinted on the swollen neon veins
on the city's sleepless brow,
on the incessant smile of a candidate
who was trying, not without difficulty, to get in
somewhere, I don't remember just where,
and to the snow it didn't matter where.

But in the Park it fell undisturbed:
the snowflakes descended cautiously
onto the softly sinking leaves,
soggy multicolored floats;
onto a pink and tremulous balloon
childishly fastened with chewing gum

to the trunk of an evergreen
and sleepily rubbing its cheek against the sky;
onto someone's forgotten glove,
onto the zoo, which had shown its guests out,
onto the bench with its wistful legend:
PLACE FOR LOST CHILDREN.

Dogs licked the snow in a puzzled way,
and squirrels with eyes like lost beads
flickered between cast-iron baskets,
amidst trees lost in the woods of themselves.
Great juttings of granite stood about
morosely, preserving in mineral calm
a silent question, a reproach—
lost children of former mountains.

Behind a wire fence, zebras munching hay
peered, at a loss, into striped darkness.
Seals, poking their noses from the pool,
caught snow in mid-flight on their whiskers;
they gazed around them, quizzical, confused,
forsaken children of Mother Ocean
taking pity, in their slippery style,
on people—lost children of the Earth.

I walked alone. Now and then, in the thicket,
the crimson firefly of a cigarette
floated before an unseen face—
the staring pupil of Night's wide eye.

And I felt some stranger's feeling of being lost
was searching embarrassed
for a feeling of being lost like my own,
not knowing that this is what I longed for.

At night, beneath this snowfall,
its whispered secret having made us one,
America and I sat down together
in the place for lost children.

Translated by John Updike with Albert C. Todd

GENTLENESS

This can't go on:
is after all injustice of its kind.
How in what year did this come into fashion?
Deliberate indifference to the living,
deliberate cultivation of the dead.
Their shoulders slump and they get drunk sometimes
and one by one they quit,
orators at the crematorium
speak words of gentleness to history.
What was it took his life from Mayakovsky?
What was it put the gun between his fingers?
If with that voice of his, with that appearance,
if ever they had offered him in life
some crumbs of gentleness.
Men live. Men are trouble-makers.
Gentleness is a posthumous honor.

Translated by Robin Milner-Gulland and Peter Levi, S. J.

BABII YAR *

No monument stands over Babii Yar.
A drop sheer as a crude gravestone.
I am afraid.
                    Today I am as old in years
as all the Jewish people.
Now I seem to be
                    a Jew.
Here I plod through ancient Egypt.
Here I perish crucified, on the cross,
and to this day I bear the scars of nails.
I seem to be
                    Dreyfus.
The Philistine
                    is both informer and judge.
I am behind bars.
                    Beset on every side.
Hounded,
            spat on,
                    slandered.
Squealing, dainty ladies in flounced Brussels lace
stick their parasols into my face.
I seem to be then
                    a young boy in Byelostok.
Blood runs, spilling over the floors.
The bar-room rabble-rousers

give off a stench of vodka and onion.
A boot kicks me aside, helpless.
In vain I plead with these pogrom bullies.
While they jeer and shout,
                    "Beat the Yids. Save Russia!"
some grain-marketeer beats up my mother.
O my Russian people!
                    I know
                              you
are international to the core.
But those with unclean hands
have often made a jingle of your purest name.
I know the goodness of my land.
How vile these antisemites—
                    without a qualm
they pompously called themselves
"The Union of the Russian People"!
I seem to be
          Anne Frank
transparent
          as a branch in April.
And I love.
          And have no need of phrases.
My need
          is that we gaze into each other.
How little we can see
                    or smell!
We are denied the leaves,
                    we are denied the sky.
Yet we can do so much—

                    tenderly
embrace each other in a dark room.
They're coming here?
                         Be not afraid. Those are the booming
sounds of spring:
                    spring is coming here.
Come then to me.
                         Quick, give me your lips.
Are they smashing down the door?
                                        No, it's the ice breaking . . .
The wild grasses rustle over Babii Yar.
The trees look ominous,
                         like judges.
Here all things scream silently,
                              and, baring my head,
slowly I feel myself
                    turning gray.
And I myself
              am one massive, soundless scream
above the thousand thousand buried here.
I am
      each old man
                    here shot dead.
I am
      every child
                    here shot dead.
Nothing in me
              shall ever forget!
The "Internationale," let it
                         thunder

when the last antisemite on earth
is buried forever.
In my blood there is no Jewish blood.
In their callous rage, all antisemites
must hate me now as a Jew.
For that reason
                I am a true Russian!

Translated by George Reavey

FEARS

Fears are dying out in Russia
like the ghosts of bygone years,
and only like old women, here and there,
they still beg for alms on the steps of a church.

But I remember them in their strength and power
at the court of triumphing falsehood.
Like shadows, fears crept in everywhere,
and penetrated to every floor.

Gradually, they made people subservient,
and set their seal upon all things:
they taught us to shout when we should have kept silent,
and to shut our mouths when we had need to shout.

Today all this has become remote.
It's strange even to recall nowadays
the secret fear of being denounced,
the secret fear of a knock at the door.

And what of the fear of speaking to a foreigner?
A foreigner's one thing, but what of speaking to one's wife?
And what of the boundless fear of remaining
alone with silence after the brass bands have stopped?

We were not afraid of building in the blizzard,
or of going into battle while shells exploded,
but at times we were mortally afraid
of even talking to ourselves.

We were not corrupted or led astray;
and Russia, having conquered her fears,
gives rise—not without reason—to even
greater fear among her enemies!

I wish that men were possessed of the fear
of condemning a man without proper trial,
the fear of debasing ideas by means of untruth,
the fear of exalting oneself by means of untruth,

the fear of remaining indifferent to others,
when someone is in trouble or depressed,
the desperate fear of not being fearless
when painting on a canvas or drafting a sketch.

And as I write these lines—
and I am in too great a haste at times—
I have only one fear when writing them:
the fear of not writing with all my power.

Translated by George Reavey

TALK

You're a brave man they tell me.
                                    I'm not.
Courage has never been my quality.
Only I thought it disproportionate
so to degrade myself as others did.
No foundations trembled. My voice
no more than laughed at pompous falsity;
I did no more than write, never denounced,
I left out nothing I had thought about,
defended who deserved it, put a brand
on the untalented, the ersatz writers
(doing what had anyhow to be done).
And now they press to tell me that I'm brave.
How sharply our children will be ashamed
taking at last their vengeance for these horrors
remembering how in so strange a time
common integrity could look like courage.

Translated by Robin Milner-Gulland and Peter Levi, S. J.

BIRTHDAY

Momma, let me congratulate you on
the birthday of your son.
You worry so much about him. Here he lies,
he earns little, his marriage was unwise,
he's long, he's getting thin, he hasn't shaved.
Oh, what a miserable loving gaze!
I should congratulate you if I may
momma on your worry's birthday.
It was from you that he inherited
devotion without pity to this age
and arrogant and awkward in his faith
from you he took his faith, the Revolution.
You didn't make him prosperous or famous,
and fearlessness is his only talent.
Open up his windows,
let in the bird-song from the leafy branches,
kiss his eyes open.
Give him his notebook and his ink bottle,
give him a drink of milk and watch him go.

Translated by Robin Milner-Gulland and Peter Levi, S. J.

COLORS

When your face
appeared over my crumpled life
at first I understood
only the poverty of what I have.
Then its particular light
on woods, on rivers, on the sea,
became my beginning in the colored world
in which I had not yet had my beginning.
I am so frightened, I am so frightened,
of the unexpected sunrise finishing,
of revelations
and tears and the excitement finishing.
I don't fight it, my love is this fear,
I nourish it who can nourish nothing,
love's slipshod watchman.
Fear hems me in.
I am conscious that these minutes are short
and that the colors in my eyes will vanish
when your face sets.

Translated by Robin Milner-Gulland and Peter Levi, S. J.

ZIMA JUNCTION*

So years went past, one after the other.
I grew up in the small town
acquiring an affection for the forest
and landscape and the quiet houses.
I grew up
   and at hide-and-seek
uncatchable whatever guard you kept
we peered out from the barn through bullet-holes.
There was war at that time;
Hitler not far from Moscow.
      And we
—we were children and accepted a lot lightly.

From classroom threats untroubled and forgetful
we tore away out of the school playground
and ran down through fields to the river,
broke open a money-box and ran away
to look for the green mare,
baited our wet hooks.
I used to go fishing, stuck páper kites,
or often wandering by myself bare-headed
sucked at clover, grass polished my sandals,
I know the black acres the yellow hives

---

 * This excerpt is from one of Yevtushenko's most famous poems. In the English edition (*Selected Poems*, 1962), it runs to 30 pages.

the luminous clouds that dropped still lightly stirring
half out of sight behind the immense horizon,
and skirting around outhouses used to listen
for the neighing of the horses, peacefully
and tiredly fell asleep in old hayricks
long darkened by the rain.

I scarcely had one care in the world,
my life, presenting no big obstacles,
seemed to have few or simple complications—
life solved itself without my contributions.
I had no doubts about harmonious answers
which could and would be given to every question.
But suddenly this felt necessity
of answering these questions for myself.
So I shall go on where I started from,
sudden complexity, self-generated,
disturbed by which I started on this journey.

Into my native forest among those
long-trodden roads I took this complication
to take stock of that old simplicity,
—like bride and groom, a country matchmaking.
So there stood youth and there childhood together,
trying to look into each other's eyes
and each offending, but not equally.
Each wanted the other to start talking.
Childhood spoke first, "Hullo then.
It's your fault if I hardly recognized you.
Once when I often used to dream about you

I thought you'd be quite different from this.
I'll tell you honestly, you worry me.
You're still in very heavy debt to me."
So youth asked if childhood would help,
and childhood smiled and promised it would help.
They said good-bye, and, walking attentively,
watching the passers-by and the houses,
I stepped happily, uneasily out
through Zima Junction, that important town.

I worked things out about it in advance
—and just in case—with these alternatives,
if it hadn't got any better then it wouldn't
have got any worse.
Somehow the Corn Exchange had got smaller,
so had the chemist shop, so had the park;
it was as if the whole world were smaller
than it was when I left it.
And it was hard at first among other things
to see the streets hadn't all got shorter,
but I was walking with a longer pace
ranging the town.

Translated by Robin Milner-Gulland and Peter Levi, S. J.

BOMBS FOR BALALAIKAS

Again, again, again.
Blood, blood, blood.
Through Sol Hurok's office I walk.
By my side, their dignity unharmed,
two anecdotes of black humor:
two detectives
                guarding me.
Two detectives guiding me,
                        a Russian poet.
Someone's portraits crunch under foot.
Something crunches in my heart as well:
Art comes cheap no longer
when an innocent being
pays for it with her life.
Who are you,
                murderers, faces unseen?
Bombing art.
                What a refinement of taste!
If art must be protected
from you by the police,
                        you're bastards!

Today someone phoned Barry Boys.
An OK guy
                and a marvelous actor:

"Refuse

      or it will be too late!

to appear tomorrow

        with the Red Commissar!"

Barry,

     nevertheless you and I are alive.

Barry, my old friend,

          nevertheless you and I are older

than this girl, cut down in pain,

this innocent secretary, guilty of nothing.

Poor Iris,*

     victim of the age,

you've fallen,

       fragile,

       dark-eyed

Jewish girl suffocated by smoke,

as though in a Nazi gas chamber.

It's hard to vent out poisoned air.

The stench of Auschwitz

       and Babii Yar.

If Tchaikowsky were alive

       and here—

would they also call him "commissar!"?

How many friends of yours

      Solomon, Son of Israel,

in frames on your office walls!

*Iris Kones, a 27-year-old receptionist in Sol Hurok's New York office, was killed by the bombing on January 26, 1972.

148

And on the floor

        Stanislavsky with his wounds.

Near by

     Plisetskaya

        half on fire.

There, where the damned bomb went off,

besides somebody's earrings

          booms a basso,

a portrait of Chaliapin inscribed,

           "To you, Sol . . ."

Give me some fresh air!

        It terrifies, sickens.

I must speak out:

What are the sins

      of poetry and music?

Of accordions

     and violins?

Who are you—

      whose faces are hidden now?

Are songs and dances

      propaganda?

You're anti-Russian

     anti-Semitic

anti-American!

You want to play tricks?

You want for the house of art

      as for the house of God

bombs — bombs

    for balalaikas,

and hatchets for the feet
                of ballerinas?
Put on your masks to fool the guards
For the sake of a cheap thrill
tomorrow, with a knife,
                you'll cut Oistrakh's strings,
and the day after tomorrow—
                into the side of Rostropovich!
Damn you, servants of hell
who seek coexistence between peoples
by building bridges of cadavers.
Applause is the right noise for art—
You haven't the strength
                to muffle the explosions
                    of love.

America, honest America
is rising to defend the arts
                of Russia.
I sing an ode to you,
              angel of art!
Above the madmen,
              above the lepers,
fly forever
        from people to people
with wings singed by fire.

Translated by Stanley Kunitz with Albert C. Todd

DWARF BIRCHES

We are dwarf birches.
We sit firmly, like splinters,
under the nails of frosts

and the Khanate* of Eternal Freeze
engages in many shenanigans
to bend us down lower and lower.
Are you astonished, Parisian chestnuts?

Are you pained, haughty palms,
that we seem to have fallen low?
Are you embittered, pacesetters of fashion,
that we are all such hunchbacks?

While safe and warm, though,
you are pleased with our courage,
and you send us, pompous and mournful,
your moral support.

You figure, dear colleagues of ours,
that we are not trees but cripples.
Yet, our leaves—though ugly—
seem progressive to you, for the frost.

*Khanate: Khau, medieval Mongol sovereign.

Thanks a million. Alone, if you please,
we shall weather it under the sky,
even if savagely bent and twisted.
Without your moral support.

Of course, you command more freedom.
But, for all that, our roots are more strong.
Of course, we don't dwell in Paris,
but we are valued more in the tundra.

We are dwarf birches.
We have cleverly made up our poses.
But all this is largely pretense.
Constraint bears the form of rebellion.

We believe, bent down forever,
eternal frost can't last.
Its horror will yield.
Our right to stand upright will come.

Should the climate change, won't
our branches at once grow
into shapes that are free?
Yet, we're now used to being maimed.

And this worries and worries us,
and the frost twists and twists us,
but we dig in, like splinters,
we—dwarf birches.

1972   *Translated by Vera Dunham*

BELLY DANCE

By the dispassionate pyramids
under the clicking of tongues,
there rose her belly—
the pitiful yolk of a yellow moon.
It rose in front of sucking eyes,
lewd and coarse winks.
It hung over pilaf
                        and bottles,
over the howling men,
                        their thick necks,
over fat,
        over greasy mouths,
                        over bellies . . .
And the pharaoh belly-power
spilled over from the fullness
of feeling and filth.
Howling and growling
with pleasure,
they looked on
as if she were a slave.
They watched
the sweaty belly of a worker
devour itself.

Squinting a frightened eye,
the belly spun like a top

spilling the woman on the floor
now flat on her back
now face down.

The belly drew itself in like a moan.
A fish flailing with its tail
against the net of derision,
the crazed belly
flung against the floor
its woman's head.

The belly enacted fever.
It staged birth. It trembled
as if a stuck dagger was forced
deeper and deeper.

The belly was seized and twisted
as if hunger held it in its grip.
The artist had grown up in hunger.
And life is the yardstick of craft.

Well, later in the sad hotel room,
in the dusk of numb dawn,
her small slipper was crushed
by a shoe made in New York.

Work was leaving her body
while the soul came in slowly.
She liked him. There was something to him.
She would not have said yes just like that.

A restless spirit, half the world
he had criss-crossed time and again.
With the drug of excitement
he hoped to still his pain.

He had known the all-knowing woman.
He possessed, one might say, largesse.
And it's only by accident he had not slept
with a dancer like this.

But in vain, morose lecher,
did he wait for the sweets of the East,
for sighs new and quite special,
for the ancient Egyptian style.

Her body turned peaceful and quiet.
All of its surface had died.
Only inside there raced, other-worldly,
the hidden tremor of stars.

As if dreaming, she touched her own belly
with the hand of a child.
A tomb it was, her belly,
for the children killed by the dance.

She was too worn out to make love.
Her lips barely moved.
She felt pure joy from her belly
that had come to rest.

Beirut, 1968   *Translated by Vera Dunham*

WAITING

My love will come
will fling open her arms and fold me in them,
will understand my fears, observe my changes.
In from the pouring dark, from the pitch night
without stopping to bang the taxi door
she'll run upstairs through the decaying porch
burning with love and love's happiness,
she'll run dripping upstairs, she won't knock,
will take my head in her hands,
and when she drops her overcoat on a chair,
it will slide to the floor in a blue heap.

Translated by Robin Milner-Gulland and Peter Levi, S.J.

THANKS

To Yu. Lubimov

Say thanks to your tears.
Don't hurry to wipe them.
Better to weep and to be.
Not to be is to die.

To be alive—bent and beaten.
Not to vanish in the dark of the plasm.
To catch the lizard-green minute
from creation's cart.

Bite into joy like you bite
$\qquad$ a raddish.
Laugh as you catch the knife's blade
Not to be born that's what's
$\qquad$ frightening
even if it's frightening that you
$\qquad$ live.

He who is—is already lucky.
Life is a risky card.
To be drawn—that's a cocky occasion.
It's to draw a straight flush.

In the sway of wild cherry blossoms,
drunk on all, drunk on nothing,

don't shake off the large wonder
of your entrance upon the scene.

Don't count on pie in the sky.
Don't offend the earth by bitching.
For a second life cannot be
as the first did not have to be.

Don't trust decay. Trust the flare-up.
Sink into milkwood and feathery grass.
Pile the universe on your back
without cajoling too much.

Don't be a show-off in grief.
Even on the ruins of your soul,
dirty and tethered, like Zorba,
celebrate shame. And dance!

Thanks to the blackest cats
whom you hated askance.
Thanks to all the melon peels
on which you slipped.

Thanks to the fiercest of pains
for it kept giving.
And thanks to the shabbiest fate.
After all, it has come.

1969   *Translated by Vera Dunham*